RICK STEVES' EUROPEAN FESTIVALS

INTRODUCTION

IN EVERY PART OF EUROPE and in every season, in big cities and in remote villages, people embrace life through festivals. They celebrate the season, show faith with religious rituals, and honor their history. They enjoy fun-loving opportunities to dress in traditional costumes, wave their national flags, gorge on delicious feasts, and lubricate themselves with the local drink. All of it may just be an excuse for the very human need to celebrate family, friends, and culture.

In this book, we'll explore the roots of festivals and cover my top 10 favorites. Each of these colorful celebrations combines several or more of these characteristics: religious, crazy, patriotic, cultural, social, competitive, and exciting.

Here they are, in calendar order:

Venice is tops for Carnevale fun, with elaborately costumed participants posing and partying around the city, making the most of Mardi Gras before the sobriety of Lent puts a stop to the revelry.

During the Holy Week that leads up to Easter, Sevilla hosts long processions of ornate floats honoring Christ and Mary, accompanied by candle-carrying worshippers thronging the streets.

Easter is a joyous celebration, especially in Greece, where Easter eve comes with midnight fireworks and Sunday's meal is a lamb on a spit, enjoyed with extended family.

For Sevilla's April Fair, everyone gets dressed up—especially the women, who wear bright, flouncy dresses—to socialize, dance, and party, fueled by sherry.

Siena's frenetic horse race called the Palio is an exhilarating mad dash in the main square. Who will win? Thousands will witness, pray for, and bet on the results.

When the bulls and people are running in Pamplona, it's thrilling. Eager spectators—often tipsy from all-night parties—gather every morning to cheer on the thundering stampede.

On France's Independence Day—Bastille Day—any French town will offer the traveler plenty of patriotic fun, but the grandest fireworks and festivities are in Paris.

OPPOSITE (CLOCKWISE):

HOLY WEEK: *White-robed penitents lead the massive marathon parades in Sevilla.*

CARNEVALE: *Atmospheric Venice is the perfect setting for this Europe-wide party.*

OKTOBERFEST: *Thousands of beer drinkers pack Munich's pop-up beer halls.*

EASTER: *In Greece, people pray, then party.*

APRIL FAIR: *Sevillanos in costume promenade past rows of party tents.*

CHRISTMAS (center): *The season begins in Norway with angelic bringers of light.*

Towns all over Scotland proudly host Highland Games in summer. In the smaller towns, even visitors are welcome to compete. If you've ever wanted to toss a caber (giant log), here's your chance.

Munich's Oktoberfest is probably Europe's biggest party, with huge beer-hall tents that accommodate thousands of happy beer-drinkers enjoying hearty food, dancing, and oompah bands.

And the Christmas holiday season keeps much of Europe festive for a month of special events—from Santa Lucia Day (December 13) to Epiphany (January 6).

Also, to give you a broader look at Europe's many festivals, I invited my Facebook readers to contribute their favorites. You'll find their top 30 in this book.

These festivals are just a small sampling of the many, colorful events that carbonate Europe's cultural calendar. Every country has national heroes (and patron saints in Catholic countries) to honor; historic events to commemorate; and major products to celebrate (think of truffle festivals in Italy or tulip parades in

Blow off your neat itinerary if a festival comes your way.

the Netherlands). Festivals featuring the arts, dance, films, and music are held in every major city—if you search online for "jazz festival" and "Venice," you'll have a jazz festival in Venice to look forward to.

Whatever your interest, Europe likely has a festival devoted to it. I hope this book inspires you to seek out more festivals, either in Europe or your side of the Atlantic. Your only challenges are to pick your favorites and reserve your accommodations well in advance.

Then join the celebration! Cheer on the horses, bulls, dancers, and caber tossers. Quaff a mug of beer with your bratwurst while the polka plays on. As processional floats go by, marvel at the devout who carry them on their shoulders for hours. Don a mask and experience Carnevale on the world's biggest stage set, Venice. Enjoy the glad-I'm-here thrill of watching fireworks light up iconic skylines. You can call it a cultural experience . . . or you can just call it fun.

Edinburgh cuts loose during its August arts festival.

CLOCKWISE:

**RUNNING OF
THE BULLS:**
Nervous daredevils in
costume await the bulls'
release in Pamplona.

HIGHLAND GAMES:
He-men strut their
stuff in these traditional
Scottish competitions.

PALIO: Medieval Siena
stages a centuries-old
horse race.

BASTILLE DAY: In
France, the spirit of the
Revolution lives on.

European Festivals at a Glance

RICK'S TOP 10 FAVORITES

CARNEVALE, in Venice, Slovenia, Luzern, usually mid-February. *Enjoying Mardi Gras with parties, costumes, and craziness.*

HOLY WEEK, in Sevilla, Spain, week before Easter. *Processions of elaborate floats honoring Mary and Christ.*

EASTER, in Napflio, Greece. *Celebrating the Resurrection with fireworks, family, and a lamb on a spit.*

APRIL FAIR, Sevilla, two weeks after Easter. *Dressing up colorfully, drinking sherry, and partying in tents.*

PALIO, in Siena, Italy, July 2 and August 16. *No-holds-barred horse race with neighborhood pride at stake.*

RUNNING OF THE BULLS, in Pamplona, Spain, July 6-14. *People running with bulls—thundering, fast, and furious.*

BASTILLE DAY, in Paris, France, July 14. *Grand display of national pride in a proud country.*

HIGHLAND GAMES, in Airth, Scotland, later in July. *Scottish competition of feats of prowess and grace.*

OKTOBERFEST, in Munich, Germany, late September to early October. *Beer-hall tents, oompah music, hearty food, rides, and revelry.*

CHRISTMAS, in Norway, Nürnberg, Rome, France, Swiss Alps, Dec 25. *Celebrating the season with lights, markets, food, family, and traditions.*

Notes: Festivals are listed in calendar order. For festivals held across an entire country (like France's Bastille Day) or across Europe (such as Carnevale and Christmas), the particular city or country where Rick celebrated is noted above.

TRAVELERS' FAVORITE FESTIVALS

These festivals were submitted by my Facebook readers.

BATTLE OF THE ORANGES, in Ivrea, Italy, usually in mid-February. *Festive food fight remembering medieval rivalries.*

FALLAS FESTIVAL, in Valencia, Spain, on March 15-19. *Street parties and parades of giant mannequins.*

ST. PATRICK'S FESTIVAL, in Dublin, Ireland, on March 17. *Beer, Irish jigs, and all things green.*

KING'S DAY, in Amsterdam, Netherlands, on April 27. *National birthday party, celebrating canalside dressed in orange.*

BELTANE FIRE FESTIVAL, in Edinburgh, Scotland, on April 30. *Pagans dancing around roaring bonfires.*

TREE BLOSSOM FESTIVAL, in Werder, Germany, in early May. *Enjoying local fruit wines amid flowering trees.*

FESTIVAL OF FLOWERS, throughout Italy, during May and June. *Street-size mosaics made of flowers.*

MEISTERTRUNK FESTIVAL, in Rothenburg, Germany, in late May or early June. *Medieval soldiers parading and heroically chugging local wine.*

VOGALONGA, in Venice, Italy, in late May or early June. *A "protest-ival" of rowing contests in colorful garb.*

DECORACTION, in Madrid, Spain, in mid-June. *Arts and decorated facades in a neighborhood.*

VIENNA PRIDE, in Vienna, Austria, in mid-June. *LGBTQ parades and balls benefiting AIDS.*

BLOOMSDAY FESTIVAL, in Dublin, Ireland, on June 16. *James Joyce literary pub crawl.*

MUSIC FESTIVAL, in Paris, France, on June 21. *Music in countless venues across town.*

ST. JOHN FESTIVAL, in Porto, Portugal, on June 23. *Sardines, port, and head-bonking.*

NIGHT OF ST. JOHN, in A Coruña, Spain, on June 23. *Sardines, beer, and scaring off witches.*

LIGHTS OF BEAUNE, in Beaune, France, from late June to late September. *World-class wines, cuisine, and light shows.*

Karlovy Vary International Film Festival, in Karlovy Vary, Czech Republic, in early July. *International films and red-carpet events.*

Gărâna Jazz Festival, in Gărâna, Romania, in early July. *High-quality jazz in rustic mountain village.*

Bohemia Jazz Fest, in Prague, Czech Republic, in mid-July. *Laid-back jazz in atmospheric Old Town Square.*

Battle of the Archers, in Fivizzano, Italy, in mid-July. *Medieval Tuscan archery contest.*

Ludwigsburg Festival Classic Open Air & Fireworks, in Ludwigsburg, Germany, in mid-July. *Lite classical music with picnics and fireworks.*

Redentore Festival, in Venice, Italy, later in July. *Pontoon bridge across canal, lit by fireworks.*

Cosmo Jazz Festival, in Chamonix, France, in late July. *Très cool tunes in chic alpine town.*

Sighişoara Medieval Festival, in Sighişoara, Romania, in late July. *Medieval wenches, knaves, and troubadours in quirky old village.*

Edinburgh Festival, in Edinburgh, Scotland, in August. *World-class music, dance, theater, and comedy—plus bagpipes.*

Villacher Church Day, in Villach, Austria, in early August. *Oompah music, sausages, and beer without the Oktoberfest craziness.*

Festival of Gràcia, in Barcelona, Spain, in mid-August. *Neighborhoods competing for most creatively decorated street.*

Almabtrieb Festival, in Mayrhofen, Austria, in early October. *Well-dressed herds, and partying till the cows come home.*

Eurochocolate Festival, in Perugia, Italy, in mid-October. *Chocolate, chocolate, chocolate. Nuff said.*

Escalade Festival, in Geneva, Switzerland, in mid-December. *Reenactment of historic battle, with torches and bonfires.*

European Festivals

FINLAND

NORWAY
⊛ Oslo ⊛
⑩

Stockholm ⊛
SWEDEN

RUSSIA

⊛ Tallinn
ESTONIA

LATVIA
⊛ Riga

SCOTLAND
Airth ⑧
⑮ ⑳ Edinburgh
HIGHLAND GAMES

North Sea

DENMARK

⊛ Copenhagen

Baltic Sea

LITHUANIA
Vilnius ⊛

RUSSIA

⊛ Minsk
BELARUS

N. IRE.

Dublin ⑬ ㉒
IRELAND

WALES

ENGLAND

London ⊛

Berlin ⊛
⑯ Werder

Warsaw ⊛

POLAND

UKRAINE

NETHER-
LANDS

⑭ Amsterdam

GERMANY

Karlovy
Vary
㉗

Prague ㉙

CZECH REP.

MOLDO

Brussels ⊛
BELGIUM
LUX.

Nürnberg
Rothen-
burg ⑱

⑩

SLOVAKIA

Paris ⑦ ⑩
㉓
**BASTILLE
DAY**

🍺
OKTOBERFEST

Sighișoara

⊛ Vienna

Bucares

Atlantic
Ocean

Beaune ㉖

Ludwigs-
burg ㉛

Luzern

Munich
⑨

㉑ Vienna

AUSTRIA

HUNGARY

ROMANIA

Gărăna
㉞

Geneva ㊵
Chamonix ㉝
SWITZ.
⑩

Mayrhofen
㊳ Villach ㊱

FRANCE

⑪ Ivrea
Fivizzano ㉚

Venice
SLOVENIA

CROATIA

㉘

A Coruña ㉕

Porto ㉔

PORTUGAL

Lisbon ⊛

RUNNING OF
THE BULLS

Pamplona ⑥

SPAIN

Madrid ⑳

㉗ Barcelona

Valencia ⑫

① ⑲ ㉜
CARNEVALE

🐎
PALIO

⑤ Siena

㊴ Perugia

⑩ Rome

⑰

ITALY

BOSNIA-
HERZ.

SERBIA

MONT. KOSOVO

MACEDONIA

ALBANIA

Adriatic
Sea

BULGARIA

GREECE

Aegean Sea

Sevilla
② ④
HOLY WEEK

✝

Balearic Sea

APRIL FAIR

GIBRALTAR

Athens ⊛

🐑 Napflio ③

**EASTER
(EQUINOX)**

MOROCCO

ALGERIA

TUNISIA

Mediterranean
Sea

N (compass)

Christmas (Solstice) — SWITZ.

RICK'S FAVORITES

TRAVELERS' FAVORITES

THE ROOTS OF FESTIVALS

Festivals—It's in Our DNA

WHILE MANY PEOPLE don't need an excuse to party, festivals give us a reason. They fill a basic human need shared by all of us *homo sapiens*.

Festivals are public commemorations, whether solemn or joyous, that mark important events. They connect us, as individuals, to the world around us. It helps bind us to our families. It's when extended families—grandpas, cousins, and in-laws—gather together to celebrate. Like it or not, they eat and drink together, attend community events as a family, and catch up. In the process, it also unites the various generations—a time when grandma, mom, and daughter get together to bake traditional foods, or grandpa shows the grandkids how to hoist the flag for the parade. These kids will learn from the previous generation and pass on their knowledge to the next generation. This continuity shores up the familial infrastructure needed to raise the next generation and ensure the survival of the species.

In a larger way, festivals unite communities, regions, and nations. By honoring common traditions, the community is reminded of what makes their particular town or nation unique. It stokes the pride and cultural identity that can carry a people through times of war and oppression. They're reminded of their rich her-

LEFT: *Families connect during Palm Sunday rituals.*

RIGHT: *Food is a common denominator that unites all generations.*

itage, which in the case of Europeans can stretch back not merely decades but centuries.

Time-honored rituals are a familiar comfort at festival time. This is the day when we always do this, we always eat that, and we spend time with certain people. It's the time when people get out their traditional clothes—whether Bavarian lederhosen or flamboyant flamenco dresses. They pick up their folk instruments and sing the old tunes everyone knows. In Scotland, they dance the Highland Fling, and in France they belt out the "Marseillaise." Festivals always bring out the community pageantry, like parades, flags, music, and people in costume. And there's a time to just grab a beer and party in the streets.

While every festival is different, there's usually one common denominator—food. People celebrate most when they gather together to eat and drink. It's no coincidence that the word "festival" comes from the same etymological root as the word for . . . "feast."

On a personal level, festivals create lifelong memories and help give meaning to our lives. It's a chance to remember the importance of loved ones. It's a time to reflect on the seasons of life—from childhood to adulthood to old age. Annual celebrations serve as mile markers that regulate our daily lives. In the widest sense, these regularly recurring festivals make us aware of the swift and slippery passage of time, and help us find our place in the course of our existence.

But enough of that! We all know the main reason that festivals exist—to have fun!

Festivals give everyone a mandatory reason to blow off work for a while and recharge their batteries. It forces dour Dickens to give poor Bob Cratchit a day off. Way, way back in a more primitive era—that is, before the Internet, TV, and movies—you actually needed a community of flesh-and-blood people gathered together in order to have fun. Holiday time brings out the deep-seated human urge to join with loved ones and experience life to its fullest.

The Calendar of the Seasons

Festivals have been celebrated since the beginning of time, and in every culture. Thousands of years ago, prehistoric Celtic druids gathered at stone circles to rejoice when the life-giving sun returned each winter. In Shang Dynasty China, they set off fireworks to celebrate spring, India marked the darkest night of the year with lights, and ancient Egyptians paraded statues of the gods to thank them for the annual flooding of the Nile. From ancient Romans to New World Aztecs, Palestinian Jews, and Arabian Muslims, there have been feasts and fasts and parties and processions.

Most of these old festivals were tied to Nature's own calendar of the seasons—winter, spring, summer, and fall.

Imagine you're living in Europe in prehistoric times. The bleakness of winter . . . the short days and long nights, the mist and rain, barren fields, the hunger and the cold. You're at the mercy of nature, controlled by the fickle spirits—Odin, Thor, wood elves, and river trolls. In summer, the gods bring warmth, plants grow, and food is plentiful. Then it gets cold again, and the earth becomes frozen and forbidding. Nothing's growing. Will we all starve? Where did the sun go?

Many of today's festivals have roots that go thousands of years deep.

Druids and priests did their best to find out by tracking the course of the sun. They built impressive stone monuments (like Stonehenge in England) that lined up with the rising sun on important days, like the winter solstice (when the sun is at its lowest on the horizon) and the vernal equinox (marking the start of spring). They established a crude calendar that offered some assurance that the sun would return again. It helped them plan their lives: when to plant, when to harvest, when to get ready for the bleak winter, and when they could let their guard down for a while to party.

Even today, many European festivals still reflect their origins in the cycle of seasons. They're rooted in the course of the sun and the moon. They're tied to agricultural events like the planting, the harvest, when to pasture the cattle, and when to take them to the village for sale.

So spring became a time of joyous festivals celebrating the earth's renewal, fertility, and "rebirth." Even today, spring brings various high-spirited celebrations. In Britain, the gaily dressed Morris Dancers chase away winter, while in Italy's villages, troubadours go from farm to farm, where they're invited in to enjoy some bread, cheese, and wine—the fruits of last year's harvest. As the days get warmer, it's time to really cut loose. On the first of May, people still build bonfires and dance around them half-nekked, frolicking like pagans of old.

Summer was the time when the hard work of planting was done and the hard work of harvesting was still weeks away. Let's celebrate! On the summer solstice (the longest day of the year), ancient people rejoiced. These days, modern pagans (especially in Northern countries) still put flowers in their hair and dance around a foliage-covered maypole—a symbol of fertility—to ensure a good harvest. Summer is the time to race horses, chase bulls, and dance the Highland Fling. It's the time to stay up very late drinking lots of wine, sangria, or whisky.

When autumn comes, it's the season to give thanks for a bountiful harvest. Throughout Europe, there are still many harvesting festivals, particularly the joyous grape harvest. In France, they debut the new Beaujolais wine to carry the joy into the coming winter. In alpine regions, men in lederhosen and women in dirndls parade flower-bedecked cows through the streets to celebrate the annual return from the mountain pastures. In Bavaria, they still dress in their traditional garb to drink beer, feast on the first fruits of the harvest, and celebrate their peasant heritage at Oktoberfest.

As winter settles in and days get dark, some festivals have a solemn aspect—it's a time to reflect on the year. But people also take the occasion to light fires and

OPPOSITE:

Following the seasons, Europeans have long celebrated spring with maypoles, summer with music, fall by harvesting grapes, and winter by cheering themselves up against the cold.

candles, to eat and drink, to sing, to make merry together, and stave off the gloom of winter. Even today, Christians welcome the birth of the Son of God much as the pagans of old did, who marked the solstice—the birth of the Sun.

The Christian Rebranding

By around A.D. 300, pagan Europe was rapidly becoming Christian. When the Roman Emperor Constantine legalized the growing religion, the once-persecuted sect soon became the largest religion in Europe.

Church leaders began rebranding pagan festivals to fit the story they wanted to tell. They scheduled their religious festivals to coincide with seasonal events that had been observed since the dawn of time. So the pagan festival of the god Saturn, which brought joy in the dead of winter, became the festive Christian holiday of Christmas. The pagan winter bacchanal became Carnevale. And the worship of Eostre—the pagan goddess of spring—became Easter, a celebration of Christ's "rebirth" in the Resurrection.

Over the next thousand years (during the Middle Ages), Europe's festivals were, at least ostensibly, Christian celebrations. In fact, the word "holiday" (from Old English) originally meant "holy day." And the word "festival" (from Latin by way of Old French) was the "feast" day of a Christian saint. Most celebrations were a kind of birthday party for beloved saints who had died as martyrs for the faith. (In fact, their "birth" day was actually the day they'd died, and thus were "born" into eternal life.) Over the years, other saints were added: popes, bishops, writers and teachers, and those who devoted their lives to working with the poor, sick, and downcast. Eventually, the Christian calendar became stuffed with some 10,000 honored saints, each with their special day.

These saints were revered by towns and villages who bonded with them and held festivals in their honor. The saint might have personal meaning to them. Saint Fermín put Pamplona, Spain, on the map. George who slayed dragons

Many ancient festivals took their current form in medieval times, when Christianity dominated Europe.

looked out for Barcelona. Saint Mark visited Venice, and the Virgin Mary protected Siena. When their saint's day came around, they'd be sure to hold a big community festival.

For a thousand years or more, this Christian calendar dictated Europe's festivals. It established the various prayers and Bible readings throughout the year—from Jesus' birth (Christmas) to death and resurrection (Easter) to Ascension and Pentecost. And the "feast" days of the saints always gave people a great excuse to break out food, drink, costumes, and musical instruments, and . . . to feast.

THE NEW RELIGION—SECULARISM

With the coming of the modern secular world, the calendar of festivals grew yet again.

There was a new religion in town—government. New festivals arose to mark the symbolic birth of nations. Every European country has its "Fourth of July" day to mark its coming-of age. There's Bastille Day in France (July 14), Portugal's independence from Spain (December 1), Sweden's election of King Vasa (June 6), Switzerland's federation to fight its enemies (August 1), and so on. With the rise of nationalism in the 1800s, governments established these as national holidays to remember their independence and bind the citizens together.

Other festivals arose out of secular traditions. Military exercises evolved into the sporting contests that became Scotland's Highland Games. Competitive horsemanship exercises became Siena's Palio horse race. Europe's various "changing of the guard" ceremonies—like at London's Buckingham Palace, Greece's Parliament, and even tiny Monaco—are holdovers of a time when this coordinated

Patriots everywhere celebrate their country's "Fourth of July."

Europe today has a variety of spectacles, from synchronized soldiers to colorful krishnas.

show of force helped dispel any thoughts of attack by enemies. Other festivals have arisen to mark specific historical events. In Germany, for example, a royal wedding became a reason to party every year for Oktoberfest.

In our global age, new traditions have arisen. Europeans have borrowed from and absorbed many of the festivals of its former colonies. So in the Netherlands, they celebrate the Surinamese holiday of Kwaku, while Londoners party during the Hindu Diwali festival of light. Other new festivals might celebrate a particular art or hobby, like the Cannes Film Festival and Edinburgh Festival of the arts. From Workers' May Day, to Gay Pride, to Arbor Day, to International Talk Like a Pirate Day . . . there's something for everyone.

A Journey through Europe's Festivals, in Time and Space

Now let's get started with our selection of favorite festivals.

We'll follow them in order, as they as they appear throughout the calendar year—from the dead of winter to the joy of spring to party-hearty summer to the thanksgiving of autumn—and back to the close of the year.

Our journey spans thousands of miles, across the extent of Europe. We'll see festivals from the Highlands of Scotland to the warmth of Spain, from the tops of the Alps to the lights of Paris to the remote villages of Slovenia. Along the way, we'll see the many different ways people can have fun. We'll see festivals of every stripe—seasonal, pagan, religious, political, military, historical, and so on. We'll dig deeper into the origins of the festivals, and see how they've evolved over the years. So, what may have begun as a celebration of the solstice got rebranded as a Christian saint's day. That in turn might have been conflated with the annual village fair or livestock-breeders show. Then in modern times, it might have become commercialized and transformed again as it was turned into an event fit for a mass

A Year of European Festivals

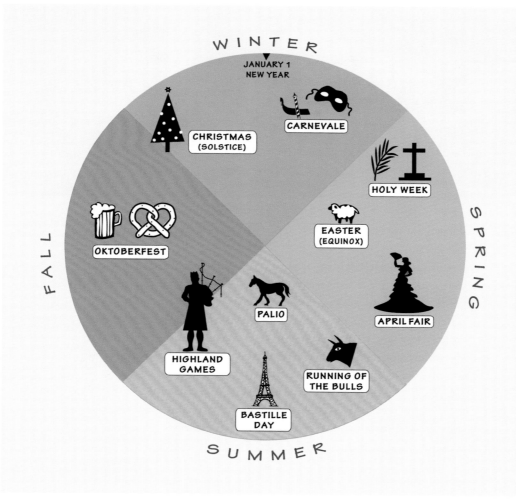

audience. Each generation has added a new spin to the traditions they've inherited from their ancestors.

In fact, most of Europe's festivals today are a crazy-quilt combination of many traditions. The genealogy of the festival gets lost in the mists of time. Today's festivals have become a weird family of pagan cousins, religious aunts, and brash kids.

And so, what was once a solemn festival honoring an ancient martyr has become a drunken orgy where people run with charging bulls. A medieval rivalry was transformed into a crazy horse race. The somber Christian festival of Holy Week has been infused with flamenco music rooted in the Muslim call to prayer. And an Easter celebration now celebrates the Lamb of God with lamb on the spit.

The traditions may have evolved, but even after all these centuries, Europe retains many of its old customs. These festivals bring people together today, and they connect them to their ancestors of long ago. People still celebrate in much the same way they've done for generations, centuries, even millennia ago. There are still age-old fertility rites—singing and dancing, throwing flowers, gorging on sweets, and giving gifts. In the Alps, fathers still bless the house as their father's father did. On Easter Eve, people still stay up awaiting the return of Jesus, just as their pagan forebears awaited the dawning of spring. They still find reason for joy in the middle of winter as the ancient Romans did 2,500 years ago. Europe still carries on traditions that date back centuries—to medieval times, to pagan Rome, to the days of the earthly Jesus, and even to the dawn of humankind.

Europe's festivals can be fun, solemn, spiritual, crazy, or primal.

CARNEVALE

Carnevale—Chasing Away Winter

It's the DOLDRUMS of winter. Late February. Gray skies, snow, rain, cold. Everyone's been trapped indoors for months now. Same old, same old. Cabin fever is setting in. So what do you do?

Throw a party!

And so it came to pass that one of Europe's oldest, biggest, and most wide-ranging festivals was born—Carnevale.

It's celebrated all over Europe. Italians (and I) call it Carnevale. Germanic countries celebrate it as Karneval, or Fasching. It's called Fastnacht in Switzerland and Vastenavond in the Netherlands, while smaller towns might have their own special name. Carnevale is now celebrated all over the world. There's the huge

Carnevale of Rio de Janeiro, while in the States—especially New Orleans—we celebrate it as Mardi Gras.

No matter where, Carnevale is a time of craziness and excess. In many places, it's a full week of music, dancing, eating, drinking, and flirting. Partiers wear masks and wacky costumes. They decorate floats and parade through the streets, amid a storm of confetti. During Carnevale, the traditional societal order is turned upside-down. Authority is challenged and rules are broken. A Prince of Fools might be given the key to the city, and a city council of faux-officials makes the rules. Joyous chaos reigns.

The Carnevale festival is very old. It's likely rooted in pagan late-winter celebrations, when people partied heartily to put on a brave face in the bleakest of seasons. This was the time of year when the stock of foods they'd stored last fall

OPPOSITE: In the dead of winter, crazy parties erupt across Europe.

RIGHT: Carnevale's indulgence ends when the fasting of Lent begins.

was running low. As the snow melted (nature's refrigerator), delicacies like fresh meat would soon be spoiling. So they feasted on it before it all went bad, knowing that spring was just around the corner, bringing fresh game and new crops. Also, the Carnevale party was a great way to put your crazy on and scare off the demons of winter.

When Christianity entered Europe, the raucous event took on another purpose. It happened to coincide with the start of the 40 days of solemnity that led up to Easter, the period called Lent. Christian authorities realized that nobody was about to give up the biggest party of the year, so Carnevale became part of the religious calendar. Carnevale was the last blow-out of eating, drinking, and rebelliousness before the fasting, sobriety, and restrictions of Lent. (The word "carnevale" literally means "farewell, meat.") The festival served as a kind of social safety-valve to let off steam after the dreariness of winter and before the enforced reverence of Easter.

Carnevale generally begins sometime in late February, one week before Lent starts. With each succeeding day, the party picks up intensity, with bigger parades, more lavish banquets, and later nights. It culminates the night before Ash Wednesday, when Lent begins. This is the day known as Shrove Tuesday, or what's called "Fat Tuesday" in French—that is, "*Mardi Gras.*"

Carnevale is one of Europe's great parties. Every city or town has a different way of celebrating. Let's start with the most famous Carnevale of all—in Venice.

VENICE'S CARNEVALE— A GLOBAL PARTY IN AN ELEGANT SETTING

Carnevale casts a spell on Venetians and visitors alike. What makes Venice's festival so unique is its long history, its partiers in elaborate masks, and the one-of-a-kind location.

The island city of Venice—laced with canals, and free of cars—is one of the

Venice's scenery becomes the stunning backdrop for parties all over town.

world's greatest natural movie sets. It's the perfect backdrop for revelers in costumes making the scene. Of course, any time of year, Venice is romantic: Gondolas glide gently down misty canals. Music plays nightly in St. Mark's Square, where people dance surrounded by fabled buildings of arches and domes. Venice is perfect for strolling down narrow, peeling-plaster alleyways, and climbing to the top of a bridge to gaze down at your reflection in a quiet canal. By February,

all this atmosphere is just waiting for a party to arrive. Venice's Carnevale is not just a celebration, it's a piece of open-air theater that draws thousands of visitors from around the world.

Venice has hosted Carnevale since at least the 13th century, when it was Europe's wealthiest and most cosmopolitan city. Visitors enjoyed spiced foods from Africa, silk clothes from Asia, and imported wine drunk from glass goblets forged by Venetian artists. Carnevale became a worldwide phenomenon, attended by English barons, African Moors, Byzantine scholars, and Muslim sultans.

By the 1700s, even as Venice was in economic decline, it still had a reputation for luxury . . . now tinged with decadence. It was Europe's fun city—where aristocrats from across Europe traveled to do the kinds of things they were forbidden to do at home. They ate and drank too much, gambled at the licensed casinos, and patronized Venice's thousands of courtesans (i.e., prostitutes). The year-round indulgence kicked up an extra notch at Carnevale. As Venice declined, so did Carnevale. But in the 20th century, the festival was spiffed up and marketed to the world, and today, Carnevale thrives.

Venice's festival unfolds across the city in a series of local events.

First, there are the posers. Theatrical types put on ornate costumes and masks, and strike poses in public places. Suddenly, St. Mark's Square is populated with

lords and ladies in silk gowns and masks, cavorting and gavotting. These people don't merely don a costume—they inhabit a role. They pose and gesture in character, moving slowly with pantomime-like motions. Of course, they choose the most striking of backdrops—under the arches of the lacy Doge's Palace, beside a weathered lion statue, or cruising in a decorated gondola.

Meanwhile, the formal parties are getting underway. Fancy palazzos along the Grand Canal or on St. Mark's Square are rented out for the night. Some parties are limited to old friends, some are open to strangers (for a fee), and some are by invitation only. And some are very expensive, with thousand-dollar-a-plate spreads. (These often draw wealthy foreign business types, resulting in an awkward affair of stiff strangers. Personal experience tells me it doesn't take a lot of money to make a good party.) Whatever the locale, Venetians make it a tradition to gather together with their friends every Carnevale. It's a time to take a break from their regimented lives to let some fun and fantasy take over.

As night falls, the back alleys come alive. Revelers—whether in fancy costumes or improvised ones or no costume at all—crowd the pubs, enjoying *cicchetti* (toothpick appetizers) and *ombras* (small glasses) of cheap wine. This is where the casual tourist can best enjoy Venice's Carnevale. Join the locals as they wander from pub to pub. It's not difficult to stumble onto an informal party erupting in a piazza that's open to almost anyone in a costume, or just a partying mood.

Caught up in Carnevale, it's easy to blink away the present and imagine you're back in Venice's glory days: Happy party-goers dance under candlelit chandeliers to Vivaldi's *Four Seasons*. Servants glide by with drinks and finger foods. The gentlemen wear powdered wigs, silk shirts with lacy sleeves, velvet coats, striped stockings, and shoes with big buckles. They carry snuffboxes with dirty pictures inside the lids. The ladies powder their hair, and pile it high. And everyone wears or carries a mask on a stick to change identity in a second.

Now, as then, decadence rules the night and reality seems a distant dream. Carnevale is a time to say farewell to your old self. For at least one night, you're free to promenade, pose, and become someone you're not. And as it was centuries ago, what happens in Venice . . . stays in Venice.

THE SLOVENIAN CARNEVALE—
PRIMAL AND UNSPOILED

Some of Europe's oldest Carnevale celebrations are found in the tiny country of Slovenia. They give a taste of what Carnevale's pre-Christian origins must have been like—as a festival to chase away the winter gloom.

Wedged between the snow-capped Alps and sunny Adriatic, Slovenia feels both Germanic and Mediterranean. You can enjoy seafood and a glass of wine while watching the sun set over the Adriatic, or visit untouristed alpine villages in the heartland. The rolling countryside is dotted with charming barns and colorfully painted beehives. And the people are some of the sweetest you'll find. Even when riled, the worst curse they can muster in their native tongue is "Three hundred hairy bears!"

OPPOSITE:
Isolated Slovenian villages germinate unusual Carnevale traditions.

RIGHT:
Kurents--the hairy Slovenian Bacchus-- search for wine.

Because Slovenian villages tend to be small and isolated, Carnevale traditions are very local and deeply engrained in the village culture. These sometimes-bizarre customs can be hard for an outsider to understand, and, frankly, hard to explain. But it's just this mix of elements that gives Slovenia some of Europe's most local and non-commercialized Carnevale traditions.

Carnevale time here is called Kurentovanje (koo-rent-oh-VAWN-yeh). Locals dress up in beast-like costumes and parade through the streets. There's drinking, games, and lots of noise. Each village in the area has its own particular costumes, cast of rowdy characters, and timeless rituals.

The star of the show is a big shaggy creature called Kurent. He's a fun-loving pagan Slavic god of hedonism—a kind of Slovenian Bacchus. His role is to scare off winter and usher in the joy of spring. This huggable beast has a bulky layer of shaggy sheepskin. He has a long red tongue, horns, a snout, whiskers, two red-ringed eyes, and wears red or green socks.

Traditionally, the participants (mostly young men) make their own Kurent costume. They work in secret, so their monster will be all the more startling when it's finally revealed. They use the stinkiest hides they can find, to make the beast smell as hideous as it looks and sounds. Next, they attach five heavy cowbells to their waist. And finishing it off, they carry a stick padded on one end with the skin of a spiny hedgehog. The whole getup can weigh 40 pounds or more.

LEFT:
Kurents welcome the next generation into the herd.

RIGHT:
I can't explain these characters—they're unique to village life.

The Carnevale parade begins. Early in the morning, the men help each other get into their costumes and set off. Imagine a pack of a dozen or more hairy beasts rampaging through town, clanging their cowbells as loudly as possible. The noise is deafening. These horned monsters traverse the entire village, making a racket, chasing away evil spirits, and trying to frighten off winter. Traditionally, the young men hoped to use the parade as an opportunity to catch the eye of a potential wife. (What girl wouldn't want a stinky monster in green socks?) Even today, young women still toss them red handkerchiefs as a token of affection, which they proudly wrap around their necks and carry on.

The Kurents clang their way from house to house. The woolly mob stands outside the door and makes a horrible racket, swinging their hips back and forth to rattle their bells. Eventually the homeowner relents and comes out to appease the savage beasts with food and drink. He hangs a sausage on the end of the Kurent chief's hedgehog-covered stick. His partners swing their hips loudly with satisfaction. Then the homeowner brings out strong drinks to keep the Kurent mob well-fueled. Everyone removes their head-pieces long enough to eat and socialize a bit. Then they're on their way to the next house.

Although guys in Kurent costumes are the most popular, there are similarly raucous characters in other villages. It might be a motley crew known only as "the uglies"—men dressed in animal skins, devil masks, and horns. There's the "peasant woman" (a dude in drag) who trundles from house to house asking for food. A group of "ploughmen" asks the farmer for permission to plow his land. They hitch their fake plow (a wagon) to some other men dressed as horses, who pull it around and ceremonially unearth a big turnip. This symbolically "wakes the soil" to bring forth bountiful crops. Then the homeowner brings out eggs and sausage and wishes the merry band good health as all look forward to a prosperous spring.

What does it all mean? The traditions are so baked into village life that even the locals can only speculate. Kurentovanje dates back at least to medieval times, and probably traces back to earlier pagan traditions. Perhaps the scary masks symbolized the demons of winter and the other characters symbolized the good forces of spring. Perhaps the homeowners sharing food was symbolic of how families had to share what they had to make it through until spring. And perhaps the merry-making was a way to give each other encouragement to carry on.

Whatever the meaning, it's clear that these rituals are very old. And the traditions get renewed every Carnevale time with each new generation of fuzzy, stinky Kurents.

Luzern's Carnevale features big-head masks.

The day starts with an orderly parade of marching bands and floats.

LUZERN—ORDERLY SWISS CHAOS

In Switzerland, the city of Luzern hosts the country's biggest Carnevale festival. It's a unique event for Switzerland—a time when the normally reserved Swiss can cut loose with a burst of anarchy.

Luzern's Carnevale specialty is wearing huge outsize head masks made out of papier-mâché. The goal is creativity and artistry, executed with the perfection of a Swiss watchmaker. Some masks are whimsical, but many have a darker edge, featuring horned devils and Gothic caricatures. There's a satirical political bite to the masks and floats that isn't normally seen in Swiss society, where everyone seems to know their place in the efficient order of things.

The other well-known element of Luzern's Carnevale is music. It seems that each neighborhood club has their own marching band like you'd see in the military. But for Carnevale, the emphasis is not on marching in perfect lockstep, following a drum major. The music is purposely raucous and slightly out-of-tune, with jazz-style improvisation that's intentionally a little rough around the edges.

The festivities begin one week before Ash Wednesday, when a big tree—the *Guggerbaum*—is erected on the main square. The next day—"Dirty Thursday"— is when the party begins. Each successive day has different parades (including a kiddie parade), a costume contest, and lots of drinking.

*By nightfall, Luzern's party
animals take over in a riot of
raucous music and crazy costumes
…that's all cleaned up by the next day.*

Day by day, the celebration builds. It culminates on Fat Tuesday with the main parade. The revelry starts well before sunrise. The driving beat of multiple parading bands wakes up the city like a mobile alarm clock. Loud, boisterous music is a traditional way to chase away the demons of winter. At first, things are pretty orderly. Everyone follows a set parade route, and spectators line up behind crowd barriers to watch. The marchers come in with their colorful floats, papier-mâché heads, and brass bands. Everyone politely applauds the creativity and artistry.

Then it gets weird. The parade splits up into smaller groups, and branches off the prescribed route. Soon they're wandering aimlessly down back alleys and generally taking over the whole city, as the party goes on and on. You're walking along and suddenly, here comes a marching band—way too drunk, wearing crazy masks, improvising, and happily off-key. They stop into a bar to fuel up, then take over the stage to spontaneously play more tunes. Then they're off to the next pub.

The whole town gets caught up in the spirit. People clog the streets. Restaurants are packed. Even five-star hotels open their doors to let the partying public celebrate inside.

As dusk settles in, all these dispersed marching bands somehow seem to find each other again. They merge together and reorganize for a long final parade. Musicians demonstrate that famous Swiss stamina, playing on and on. After the parade ends, the party continues, with the whole town dispersing once again—drinking, binge-eating, and dancing in the streets into the wee hours.

It's the perfect end to Carnevale. The always-efficient Swiss have ticked off every box of the classic Carnevale season. Outlandish masks? Check. Big parades? Check. Loud music, heavy drinking, and dancing in the streets? Check. There's even the obligatory anti-authority chaos. The thing is, all this Carnevale craziness is somehow still very Swiss. The streets are never dangerous, just filled with a relaxed vibe of goodwill. No windows get broken and no one gets hurt. And at the end, the street-sweeping machine is there to make sure everyone wakes up the next morning to perfect Swiss cleanliness and order.

HOLY WEEK IN SEVILLA

THE PASSION OF CHRIST
AND THE PASSION OF SPAIN

As Europe awakens with a massive Carnevale hangover, the calendar of festivals takes on a more somber tone. For the next 40 days and 40 nights, Europe's Christians will commemorate Lent, a period of fasting and reflection. The weeks drag by during the gray and chilly dog days of winter. This communal sobriety builds to a climax of religious pageantry in the final seven days leading up to Festivals—known as Holy Week.

Day by day throughout Holy Week, Christians recount the events of the final week in the life of prophet Jesus of Nazareth (c. 4 B.C.-c. A.D. 33). They remember his arrest, trial, suffering, and death by crucifixion. These events—full of human

Sevilla—where the solemn lead-up to Easter is observed most fervently.

drama and emotion—are known collectively as The Passion. Holy Week is celebrated most fervently in the European country known for passion, intensity, saints, mystics, and the Inquisition—Spain. The most famous celebrations are held in that most "Spanish" of cities—Sevilla.

Separated from the rest of Europe by the Pyrenees Mountains, Spain has developed a unique identity and heritage, and this is reflected in their centuries-old Holy Week traditions. Sevilla's festivities can be traced to at least 1604, and many rites go back into medieval times. Here, Holy Week (called Semana Santa in Spanish) is an epic event that stirs the soul and captivates all who participate.

The best-known events are the parades. These feature wooden floats, decorated with statues depicting the events of Jesus' last days, accompanied by hooded penitents dressed in eerie medieval-looking robes. The processions through the streets can be marathon affairs, lasting for hours on end. Some are at night, with the participants bearing torches or tall candles, or with statues lit by elaborate electric chandeliers. Every day of the week there's a different parade, focusing on a different aspect of the Passion of Christ, as the emotion builds towards Festivals.

PALM SUNDAY—THE PARADES BEGIN

Sevilla's Holy Week kicks off on the Sunday before Festivals—known as Palm Sunday. Families dress up and head to their parish church for Mass. Then, promenading with palm and olive branches, they make a loop through the neighborhood, eventually returning to their church. They're ceremonially recreating that first Palm Sunday, when Jesus arrived in Jerusalem to a hero's welcome from his followers waving branches.

Then the people of Sevilla line the city streets for the first of the grand parades. Appropriately for Palm Sunday, the star of this parade is a float with the statue nicknamed La Borriquita—the Little Donkey. The donkey statue is carrying a statue of Jesus as he rides into Jerusalem, accompanied by happy statues waving

palm branches. When they see their beloved La Borriquita, everyone knows Holy Week is officially underway. From now on, every day until Festivals, the city will be enlivened with dozens of such processions.

Sevilla has more than a hundred different floats, called *pasos*. They're decorated with colorful, painted wooden statues. Some are outfitted with actual cloth robes to complete the illusion. These tableaus of Bible scenes present the Passion in a way the average person can understand. Parents use the statues to talk to their kids about religious matters, as well as how to deal with complex emotions like suffering and grief. Over the years, the people of Sevilla get to know these statues, and form deep attachments to them. They become like family.

MONDAY—ADORING THE FLOATS

On Monday of Holy Week, literally thousands of Sevillanos line up for hours outside of the city's churches. They've come for a chance to see their favorite parade-float statues.

Until they're actually taken on parade, the statues reside in their parish

La Borriquita—the Little Donkey—carries Christ into Jerusalem, atop this beloved parade float.

churches, atop various altars. For Holy Week, they're brought down to ground level, in preparation for being mounted on the float. During that brief window of time, people are allowed to visit the churches to view the statues up close. The various statues—of Jesus, his mother Mary, the disciples, the Jewish and Roman authorities—represent the cast of characters in the epic drama known as the Passion. Seeing them so close puts people into the right mindset as they contemplate the coming week.

Crowds jam churches for a close-up look at the elaborate floats and their realistic statues that tell the story of Christ's Passion.

After Jesus arrived triumphantly on Sunday, he quickly antagonized the Jewish elders by angrily Cleansing the Temple of unscrupulous moneychangers. The authorities hired Judas, one of Jesus' closest followers, to help arrest him. As the faithful see these ultra-realistic statues, the events come to life. Black-robed Judas leans in toward Jesus with the prearranged signal to the police—a kiss. Peter reaches out to warn his master, but the look on Jesus' face says it all: He's sad at the betrayal, but realizes that this is his fate.

Each church takes charge of a different themed float. For weeks now, they've been decorating the floats lovingly. The float itself is a sturdy wooden frame used year after year. They cover it with a decorated cloth, and adorn it with flowers and rows and rows of tall candles. Huge silver candlesticks are polished until they gleam. Hundreds of flower petals have to be plucked. These are used for showering upon their statue of Mary when she takes her turn parading through the city. When the statues are mounted atop the float, they're arranged to create a realistic scene, as if the characters are interacting in a play. With all the decorations, the whole float can weigh up to 5,000 pounds. Great care is taken to make sure that the floats are perfect in every way.

The task of all this falls to ordinary people who donate their time. Each of Sevilla's 60 or so neighborhood churches has dedicated "brotherhoods" consisting of men, women, and even young children. Besides their Semana Santa duties, the brotherhoods are involved in charitable works—funding foreign missions or social causes like helping the poor. Getting the float ready for Semana Santa is more than a job. It takes on the aspect of a humble act of penitence—a labor of love.

In some ways, the star of Semana Santa is not Jesus, but his mother, known as the Virgin Mary. Sevillanos hold a special place in their hearts for Mary, and she's the most popular statue on many of the floats. Many Catholics routinely pray to Mary, seeing her as having a sympathetic ear who will intercede for them in their troubles. During Holy Week, people get a once-a-year opportunity to interact with the Virgin face-to-face—convinced she will empathize with their needs and hear their prayers. Mary knows the sorrow of ordinary mortals, because she had

Fraternal organizations donate hours of time throughout the year polishing the floats and plucking flower petals.

to experience the unspeakable sorrow of watching her son die. The Mary statues allow the faithful to see Jesus' suffering from an acutely poignant perspective—through the eyes of a grieving mother. In Sevilla, it's not just the Passion of Christ, but the Passion of Mary.

Which of the dozens of Mary statues is Sevilla's favorite? (*¿Quién es mas bonita?*) That's like asking a Spaniard "Who's your favorite *futbol* player?"—you'll get dozens of answers. Each statue evokes a different aspect of Mary's complex emotions. The Mary known as La Estrella (for her star-like halo) has jewel-like tears streaming down her face and a mouth contorted in grief. La Soledad, or solitude, conveys Mary's great loneliness after her son was gone. La Macarena is as precious as a doll, with actual human hair, arms that can move, and a lovely cloth dress. Her beautiful expression is halfway between smiling and crying. As the patron of bullfighters, La Macarena smiles for them when they win and cries for them when they're injured.

In churches throughout Sevilla, the faithful explain the statues to their children. They gaze into the statues' eyes. They whisper prayers for a sick aunt or for strength. They kiss the foot of Jesus or stroke the hand of Mary. Many weep. These emotions are just the beginning.

Before the parade, locals can meet their favorite Mary face-to-face.

Tomorrow will bring more parades and more emotion, as Holy Week builds to its dramatic climax.

TUESDAY AND WEDNESDAY—RAMPING UP THE INTENSITY

Each day of Holy Week there are parades. In Sevilla, Tuesday's parade features eight or ten of the parish churches, each with their float. Wednesday has another eight or ten, with time even set aside for a children's parade. These are massive events, attended by tens of thousands of spectators lining the streets. The parade effectively shuts down whole sections of the city for hours on end. Locals know exactly where to go to see the parade—or what streets to avoid, to carry on with their business.

Preparing for the massive parades, the city clears the streets while vendors cater to the visitors.

The city of Sevilla has put on this festival for centuries, and it always goes off like clockwork. Along the parade route, they construct temporary ramps to cover any stair steps that might cause the float-bearers to stumble. Chairs and grandstands are readied for the lucky few who'll get to sit—because they paid for the privilege. Hundreds of heavy crosses are laid along the route, ready to be

picked up by penitents and paraded through town. Incense that perfumes the air all week is sold on the street. Prime viewing balconies along the parade route are elaborately draped with red velvet or specially embroidered shawls. If you happen to be fortunate enough to have such a balcony, you're suddenly very popular, and you invite all your friends.

The city's intensive preparations sound like a lot of work, and the celebrations are solemn, but Semana Santa brings much joy to town. People pause to refuel by popping into the tapas bars. They enjoy (meatless) pre-Festivals plates like salt cod fritters, and break into spontaneous Festivals-time songs.

Sevillanos crowd the bars for drinks and tapas, while the paraders get fitted for their cone-head costumes. Let the parades begin.

Bakeries start cranking out special Semana Santa treats. There are sweet cookies and *pestiños*—deep-fried slabs of dough dusted with sugar. Another popular Lent/Holy Week treat is *torrija*, which consists of bread slices soaked in milk, battered with egg, fried up, and sweetened—like a Spanish French Toast.

Sevillanos make sure their parade costumes are ready. Tailoring shops are buzzing with customers getting last-minute fittings. Some of the shops have been producing costumes for 200 years, and much of the work is still stitched by hand. In homes all across the city, people get ready for their church's parade. Parents help their kids don costumes, as they take their place in the continuous chain of this sacred centuries-old ritual.

Holy Thursday—The Passion on Parade

Thursday is when Christ's Passion builds to high drama. This was the day when Jesus (an observant Jew) gathered his disciples to celebrate Passover—a fateful meal that became known to Christians as the Last Supper. At the meal, Jesus broke bread and gave wine—which today is still ritually observed by Christians as Communion. After the meal, Jesus was arrested, hauled before the courts, and forced to endure an all-night ordeal of interrogation and pain.

Appropriately, Sevillanos commemorate this day in a marathon way. It starts with somber services in a church draped in mourning cloth. The liturgy focuses on the sad events. The Bible makes it clear that Jesus had been brought in on trumped up charges and subjected to a kangaroo court. He was accused of blasphemy, mocked, whipped, and tortured. Christians everywhere meditate on these events. Holy Week is the time to remember that the purpose of Christ's suffering was to bring forgiveness for our own sins.

With these penitent thoughts in mind, the faithful head to the day's long parade. Think of it. These parades are the culmination of the city's religious life. It's what the brotherhoods have been preparing for all year long. Finally, the time

The Semana Santa is fervently religious. The devout gather and pray long into the night.

has come. The participants gather at their home church and get into their costumes. They pick up their float, and start making their way along the route to its finish line, the Sevilla cathedral.

It's an unforgettable spectacle. Many are dressed in robes. These are penitents (or *nazarenos*), bemoaning their sins. The most distinct feature of their getup is hard to miss—they wear pointed, cone-shaped hats, covered with a hood. Unfortunately, for most Americans, these masked figures evoke the (gulp) Ku Klux Klan. But these outfits predate the racist KKK by centuries. The original purpose of the hoods was to hide the face, so that sinners could repent in anonymity.

The penitents, carrying candles, accompany the floats through narrow alleyways. Legions of drums crack eardrums in the confined space. Kids sit wide-eyed on parents' shoulders. Other kids collect drippings of warm wax from the street, rolling it into balls for souvenirs.

Spectators are visibly moved. Some wipe away tears as they ponder Christ's suffering and sacrifice. Others recall childhood memories of witnessing these same powerful processions with their parents. Flamenco singers in the crowd, overcome with emotion, break into timeless, mournful songs (called *saetas*), as the sad statues of Jesus or weeping Mary pass by.

The penitents slowly make their way to the cathedral (then eventually back to their home church). The journey, through miles of passionate crowds, can take up to 12 hours. Strong men called *costaleros* work in shifts, carrying the floats on their shoulders or the backs of their necks. (They do use a cushion.) As a team, they bear two tons of weight. They consider the experience a great honor—not despite but because of the pain involved. They know it's easier than carrying the cross.

GOOD FRIDAY—THE FESTIVAL PEAKS

The most passionate of the Holy Week parades comes on Good Friday, the day Jesus died. It's the longest parade, with the most penitents and the most floats. It begins shortly after midnight (of Holy Thursday) and will continue all night long until the break of dawn (giving the procession its Spanish name of *La Madrugá*.)

The procession starts in silence and darkness with the brotherhood known as

Burly costaleros *silently bear the heavy floats, while penitents march humbly alongside.*

El Silencio. A small woodwind ensemble plays solemn music, announcing their arrival. Then the music stops, accentuating the utter silence. Penitents in all-black robes and pointed hats enter with their float. The crowd stays silent as they pass, lit only by candles and the flickering of cell-phone cameras. The penitents, trudging silently along the parade route, carry big, heavy wooden crosses. A float appears bearing one of the most venerated statues—Jesus del Gran Poder, or Jesus of the Great Power. It depicts Jesus, wearing a Crown of Thorns, bent down under the weight of his cruel and heavy cross, as he climbs toward his crucifixion. Beneath him and hidden from view are the *costaleros* holding up the float—similarly bent over and trudging along. Drumming bands set a somber beat. From the crowd, a flamenco singer erupts in song—a mournful, trilling wail in the night.

The star of nearly every parade is the Virgin Mary, who seems to float above her sea of worshippers.

It recalls the events of Good Friday. On that day, Jesus was sentenced to death. How should he die? "Crucify him!" shouted the rabble. "Crucify him!" The Bible does not spare us the gruesome details. Jesus was forced to carry his own cross to the execution site. He was stripped naked. The executioners threw dice to see who'd get his clothes when he was dead. They nailed him to a cross. He was placed between two common criminals, beneath a sign that mocked him with the label "King of the Jews." Through it all, Jesus bore it stoically and with love. "Father, forgive them," he prayed, "for they know not what they do." Then he cried out with a loud voice, and said simply—"It is finished."

Watching all of this from the foot of the cross was Jesus' mother, Mary.

And so it is that the emotional climax of Sevilla's Semana Santa comes with the arrival of the Virgin Mary. The most famous of them is the float of La Macarena. Clouds of incense add an air of mystery. The float enters. Borne atop the shoulders of sweating men, the float sways back and forth through the crowds, bringing the tableau to life.

Mary, ethereal and radiant, is lit by hundreds of candles. She's mourning her son, but her sorrow is a thing of beauty. She stands atop the golden float, under a canopy, dressed in white lace, with a golden halo behind her head. Lighting her way, the candles flicker and the float sways as she is carried along. Spectators lining the streets weep. Just days before they'd stood eye to eye with La Macarena, asking her for help in their time of need. Back then, she seemed fully human. Now she parades triumphant, ready to answer their prayers. As her float passes by in the warm Spanish night, a shower of flower petals rains down, as if heaven itself is thanking her for her infinite love.

EASTER IN GREECE

Easter—Europe's Season of Renewal

Holy Week—which commemorates the death of Jesus—culminates in Easter, the day he came back to life.

Easter Sunday is celebrated by Christians all across Europe.

In Rome, the Pope hosts a huge church service on St. Peter's Square for 100,000 people, plus a global audience on TV. In Florence, they set off a colorful cartful of fireworks in front of the cathedral. In Britain, kids hunt for decorated eggs and candy hidden by the Easter Bunny. In Germany the candy is brought by the Easter Hare, while in France it's the magical flying Easter Bells (or maybe it's just Mom and Dad). There are egg-tossing and egg-rolling contests. In churches big and small, people who haven't made a single appearance all year long now file in to observe the special day. And afterwards, they gather at home with their extended families for a big meal starring grandma's home cooking.

Easter is observed by tens of thousands in St. Peter's Square in Vatican City.

In Greece, you'll find elements of all these traditions, but on a super-charged scale. For many Greeks, Easter is the biggest festival of the entire year. It's a multi-day affair. Many Greeks take the entire week off work to return to their home-towns, and much of the country shuts down. There are marathon church services of great pageantry and spectacle, exploring the deepest depths of sorrow over Jesus' death, and the height of joy at his Resurrection. There are Easter eggs, special foods, and fun family time. There's a long Saturday night vigil as they await the big day, and a joyous feast on Easter Sunday, with neighborhood gatherings and dancing in the street. For Greeks, Easter—not Christmas—is far and away the most important holy day of the year, the "Feast of Feasts."

But if you're flying to Greece for Easter, make sure you check the calendar first. You see, although Greeks celebrate Easter just as other Europeans do, they do it on a completely different Sunday. Oh, and they also make Saturday into a huge deal . . . and they have totally different rituals . . . and they eat lamb-intestine stew.

GOOD FRIDAY—REQUIEM FOR A DEITY

Greece's religious festivities start in earnest on the morning of Good Friday—the day Jesus was crucified. Greeks pack the parish churches. This will be the first of several long church services that bleed into each other over the coming days.

Churches will remain open pretty much 24/7, and worshippers stream in and out as they can.

The marathon Easter service is basically a symbolic funeral for Jesus. According to the Bible, Jesus was crucified on Good Friday. His disciples removed his body from the cross, wrapped it in a shroud, and buried him in a tomb. So, at the Good Friday service, Greek women prepare the symbolic tomb, or coffin, known as the "epitaph." It can be as simple as a plywood box or an elaborate canopy. They take turns decorating the exterior with flowers, and also sprinkle flower petals inside as a resting place.

Then comes the symbolic burial. An image of Christ—usually a flat wooden icon affixed to the wall—is removed from the cross. His "body" is then taken by the priest behind the church's iconostasis—the wall of icons of the sanctuary—to wrap it in a shroud. As candles flicker, worshippers chant and pray together, awaiting the next step as the story unfolds. A cantor sings and leads the congregation and choir.

Eventually the priest re-emerges carrying the image of Jesus wrapped in its shroud. He reverently parades the shrouded icon through the congregation of mourners. The precious and now lovingly folded shroud is laid in the ceremonial coffin. One by one, other symbolic objects are also laid in the epitaph. The image of Jesus is decked in flowers. As in any funeral, loved ones file by to pay their last respects with a kiss. The mysticism—enhanced by music, incense, and tears— heightens the emotional impact. The mourning continues throughout the day.

As dusk arrives, the funeral procession starts. The coffin is lifted onto broad shoulders and carried out of the church. All over town, other churches are simultaneously performing the same funeral rituals—carrying their individual epitaphs through town. The parades converge on the main square, where it seems the entire population awaits. The bishop, flanked by the town's priests, gives an Easter message—reminding his flock why Jesus had to die and why there's reason for hope. For the most fervent faithful, the service will continue all night long.

Eggs and the "Eostre" Bunny

Besides church services, Greeks observe Easter time with things that make the season a fun time for kids. Mom hits the market to buy food, while grandpa and grandma help the children decorate Easter eggs. Greek kids love to play a game with the dyed, hard-boiled eggs. They crack their egg against somebody else's, until one of them cracks. The lucky one whose egg stays intact will have an especially blessed year.

Besides Easter eggs for the home, Greeks treasure intricately painted ostrich eggs. Churches are decorated with them at Easter time. The religious symbolism of Easter eggs is clear: Just as eggs crack open to bring new life, Jesus emerged from the tomb with new life.

Easter eggs go back to the very origins of Easter.

Of course, Easter was one of the earliest Christian holidays, dating back 2,000 years, and eggs are the perfect symbol of Jesus's Resurrection. But Easter is also

rooted in even older festivals. It's forever linked with the Jewish Passover, as Jesus was crucified during that holiday. In fact, Greeks today still call the holiday "Pascha," from the Greek word for Passover.

But the Easter festival may be even older than Passover. It may have grown out of prehistoric festivals, when pagans celebrated the arrival of spring. In Germanic lands, this was when they worshipped the Anglo-Saxon goddess of spring and the dawn, named Eostre—likely the source of our name for "Easter." Her feast day was celebrated, like modern Easter, at the first full moon after the equinox. It was seen as a time of fertility, birth, and renewal.

Eostre's companion was a magical hare. A hare that could lay eggs. (See where I'm going with this?) The hare would lay eggs and leave them as gifts to Eostre.

And so, the idea of a gift-giving, hirsute, plantigrade, phantasmagorical leporid who brings colorful eggs, candy, and other gifts to happy kids may be an Easter tradition that's thousands of years old. And if you believe that, you probably also believe in the Easter Bunny.

Families gather to crack Easter eggs as they celebrate traditions that date back to pagan rituals welcoming spring.

THE SATURDAY CHURCH SERVICE— A JOURNEY INTO HELL

On the Saturday before Easter Sunday, worshippers pack their church again. Saturday is the longest service of the entire year. It's a day of mourning. Jesus lies dead in the tomb. The Bible tells us that his disciples were grief-stricken, convinced that he was gone forever. It's the day when, in churches everywhere in the world, Christians hold somber services, with little music and dimmed lights. But the Greek service—though sorrowful at first—has a different and more hopeful twist.

Christians observe the crucifixion, burial, and subsequent rebirth of Christ.

Whereas much of Europe is Catholic or Protestant, Greeks are Eastern Orthodox. The differences date back 1,700 years, when the ancient Roman Empire split into two kingdoms—one governed from Rome, the other from Constantinople (modern-day Istanbul). As the two cultures continued on their separate trajectories, they developed different traditions. The divide hardened in the Great Schism of 1054, when the Catholic Pope and Orthodox Patriarch excommunicated each other. In 1582, the West adopted the more accurate Gregorian Calendar, while the Eastern Orthodox world stuck with the old Julian calendar. That's why Greeks celebrate Easter on a different Sunday—usually a week or two after the West.

The divide also meant different Easter traditions. So, on Holy Saturday, Orthodox worshippers enter their church, and follow their usual Orthodox routine: They drop a coin into a donation box by the door, light a candle, say a prayer, make the sign of the cross, and kiss the nearby icon. Then they enter the nave and find a place to stand, not sit. They believe standing empowers prayers. Men stand on one side and women on the other. They're surrounded by icons—pictures of

Christ and the saints on golden backgrounds. Unlike in most Western churches, Christ is not depicted in a gruesome crucifixion, but as triumphant—seated on a throne and giving a blessing, in his role as the Pantocrator, or "Ruler of All."

As the Holy Saturday service unfolds, there's always lots of spectacle. The church is draped in mourning purple, with ostrich eggs dangling from the chandeliers. The priest wears the typical long black robe, tall hat, and long beard. The beard is a sign of wisdom, experience, and respect. (Or, as one priest told me with a wink, it's to scare Americans.) The service is not complete without lots and lots of incense. This helps involve all the senses, and evokes a mystical state. Each scent conveys a different emotional message—the agony of the Passion or the ecstasy of Resurrection. Greeks joke that the only problem with non-believers is that they have "not yet enjoyed the incense."

To a confused non-Orthodox, the Saturday service may look like ZZ Top at a séance, but it tells a story. The worshippers are mourning Jesus, who lies dead in his tomb. The priest wears mournful black vestments.

The priest tosses flowers, celebrating Christ's rebirth.

But midway through the service, the tone starts to shift. You see, according to tradition, this was the day when Jesus—while his body still lay in the tomb—descended into Hades (which is an abode of the dead, rather than hell). There, he ministered to the souls awaiting resurrection. This, the Orthodox believe, is the pivotal moment when Christ defeated the devil and death.

At this point the priest changes out of his mournful black vestments and into hopeful white ones. Now much happier and more animated, he tosses flower petals over his parishioners. This lets them know that Christ has accomplished his task. The chains of hell and death have been broken, and new life is on the way. Greeks call this Saturday "The First Resurrection."

The epic church service continues outside. People spill from their churches and once again start making their way to the main square in town. Now the mood is lighter—Easter Sunday is on its way.

SATURDAY NIGHT VIGIL—A CANDLE OF HOPE

As people gather in the village square, there's a palpable sense of expectation. Similar scenes are happening all over Europe on Saturday night. It's been weeks of buildup to Easter Sunday. There was the craziness of Carnevale and the 40 days of fasting, prayer, and reflection of Lent. During Holy Week, worshippers waved palms, kissed holy statue toes, hefted floats, and wore the robes of humble penitents. The kids have dyed eggs, and parents have decorated the home with lilies, daffodils, pussy willows, and fake grass. Grandma and grandpa have been invited.

Now, it's Saturday night. In Germany, little kids are setting out their Easter nests hoping that the Easter Hare will come during the night and fill it with goodies. French children hope the flying Easter Bells will bring them chocolate Easter "fish." In Holland, neo-pagan revelers are welcoming in spring with bonfires and Heinekens. In Spain, a float depicting Mary mourning her dead son is carried slowly through the streets. In Italy, a husband prepares to surprise his wife with a new necklace playfully hidden inside a chocolate egg. In churches across Europe,

Throughout Europe, people await Easter. Neo-pagans build bonfires anticipating the sun at the equinox, while Greek Christians gather to light candles to the Son of God.

the faithful gather for meditative vigils. Meanwhile, in that timeless realm of the spiritual world, Jesus lies dead and buried in his tomb, with a big and ominous stone rolled across the entrance.

And in Greece, villagers gather in the main square. As the minutes tick down to midnight, they stand in the darkness holding unlit candles. One lit candle is brought in. The flame has come all the way from Jerusalem, from the Church of the Holy Sepulchre that marks where Jesus was buried. The flame has been flown on a jet to Athens, then distributed to towns and villages across Greece. Now in this town square it's used to light one other candle. Then that one lights another and another until the square is illuminated by a sea of flickering flames.

It's a symbol of hope—that darkness and death will be overcome by light and the Resurrection. The bishop gives a blessing. "*Christos Anesti,*" he proclaims—"Christ is risen!"

Then at the stroke of midnight—Bang! Deafening fireworks light up the sky. (Church facades all over Greece are literally pockmarked from years of Easter celebrations.) Everyone cheers. The whole scene feels more like a happy New Year's Eve than pious Easter. Everyone hugs the people around them, even total

In Greece, after the Easter vigil ends in the main square, people head home to bless their household and enjoy a middle-of-the-night family feast.

strangers. They give one another a kiss on the cheek—the traditional Easter "kiss of love."

Easter Sunday has arrived.

SUNDAY—CELEBRATION

After the fireworks and candle-sharing, everyone hurries home for a feast. It's the middle of the night, but even kids are wide-awake and happy. As families enter their homes, they raise their candle up and make a cross above their doorway. This will bless their home for the coming year.

Then they sit down for their Easter meal—that is, their first Easter meal of the day. It's a festive gathering. This is when extended families—three or four generations, cousins, and in-laws—eat together and catch up, enjoying each other's company.

The next morning, the feasting continues, with a backyard BBQ of lamb on the spit.

The star attraction of this 1:00-in-the-morning meal is a traditional thick soup made of lamb entrails called *magiritsa*. They also feast on meat, specially baked Easter breads, and hard-boiled eggs (dyed red to symbolize Christ's blood). The meal continues into the wee hours of Easter Sunday.

As the sun rises, the feasting doesn't stop—there will be another even bigger meal on Sunday afternoon. After the fasting of Lent, the solemn church services, the Passion rituals, and all the prep work, it's now time to simply kick back and enjoy.

The big fat Greek Easter dinner is typical of family feasts all across Europe, each with its signature dishes. In France, they're enjoying leg of lamb. Brits like ham, and it's herring in Scandinavia. Almost everywhere, eggs grace the table in

The Greek Easter ends in a joyous celebration of food, wine, and dancing.

some form—hard-boiled, in a soup as a starter course, or painted eggs to be used as colorful centerpieces. And dessert is always a big deal, with Easter-themed cakes, chocolate eggs, and candy.

In Greece, Easter is not Easter without a spring lamb roasted on a spit. The men start stoking the coals early in the morning, preparing a barbecue for the afternoon meal. This goes on in backyards and town squares all over Greece. To round out the menu, *kokoretsi* is also on the spit. This beloved specialty—lamb organ meat wrapped carefully in intestines and roasted to moist perfection—assures that nothing is wasted. It takes hours to get the roasting done just right—but no one's in a hurry.

The barbecue is an excuse for a party. It's an all-day affair. There's lots of drinking, singing, and dancing. There's always the traditional "burning of Judas"—a kid-friendly event where an effigy of the disgraced betrayer is set in flames with much rejoicing. Today is not a church-going day. They've had plenty of that already, hallelujah. This is the Resurrection after-party. In villages all across Greece, families are grilling lamb, going from house to house through the neighborhood to check out other people's lambs, sharing drinks, and socializing.

When the lamb's done, the meat is removed from the skewer, and laid across a chopping block. The cook pulls out a big cleaver, and in about two minutes, reduces the entire roasted lamb into platters of meat. Everyone gathers for the big Easter meal. It's lamb off the bone, lamb off the knife, lamb off the fingers. There's beer, Easter bread, wine, music, more food, more fun, more lamb. People party into the night. Eventually the whole village ends up back at the church—not praying, but dancing and singing. Together they celebrate Easter—the Resurrection of Christ, the coming of spring, and the eternal hope of rebirth.

APRIL FAIR IN SEVILLA

APRIL FAIR—AN EARLY SPRING

EUROPE GETS A JUMP-START on summer in the warm south of Spain, when April can feel like June.

The weather is ideal. It's brisk in the morning, sunny and 75°F during the day, and it stays warm late into the night. The trees are abloom with white and purple blossoms, and the air is heavy with the scent of orange trees, jacaranda, myrtle, and jasmine. This is that short window of time—after the chill of winter but before the unbearable heat of summer—when southern Spain is at its peak. In Sevilla, the capital of Andalucía, April is the time for one of the most exuberant and colorful festivals in a country known for fiestas—the gigantic *Feria de April*,

or April Fair. There are Spring Fairs throughout Spain, but nobody does it bigger or better than Sevilla.

For seven days, thousands of Sevillanos gather at a huge fairground for a round-the-clock party that would leave the rest of Europe exhausted. As if to complement the religiosity of Holy Week, Sevilla follows it up with this vibrant, secular indulgence. The April Fair is a celebration of springtime. People parade around in their finery and check each other out, and springtime flirtations fill the air. It's a time to reconnect with your family roots. It seems everyone knows everyone in what seems like a thousand wedding parties being celebrated all at the same time.

The April Fair is also a celebration of the Andalusian heritage. That means fiery flamenco music, fine horses, artful bullfights, and flamboyant clothes. It means bowls of gazpacho, the driest of sherries, and an unquenchable obsession for sliced ham.

SEVILLA—QUINTESSENTIAL SPAIN

The April Fair is Sevilla on steroids . . . and Sevilla is Spain at its most Spanish.

Any time of year, Sevilla pulses with Iberian passion. It was the fictional setting for the dashing Don Juan and the sensual Carmen. It's a place where bullfighting is still politically correct and little girls still dream of growing up to become flamenco dancers. Sevilla's old town (the former Jewish Quarter) is a maze of narrow lanes, small plazas, tile-covered patios, whitewashed houses, and wrought-iron latticework draped in flowers. The Sevilla Cathedral is the world's largest Gothic church. The Alcázar, or royal palace, survives from the days when Spain was home to the Muslim Moors. The palace's ornate decoration and lush gardens offer a thought-provoking glimpse of a graceful Al-Andalus world that once was. But the real magic of Sevilla happens when night falls. People pack the bars for drinks and tapas, and the streets teem with strollers of all ages on the evening paseo. James Michener wrote, "Sevilla doesn't have ambience, it is ambience."

The April Fair is held at a large fairground across the Guadalquivir River from downtown Sevilla. The space is transformed into a virtual city in itself, with a dozen streets paved with the distinctive yellow Andalusian sand. Over a thousand tents, called *casetas*, line the lanes. Each colorfully-striped tent will host a private party for a family, club, or association. Colorful paper lanterns are strung overhead across the streets. One section is dedicated to a wild amusement park called the Calle de Infierno—the "Street of Hell." There's an arena for performances and events. All told, the festival's footprint covers half a square mile—twice the size of the country of the Vatican.

Sevilla—with its towering cathedral and fanciful Filella building—is home to the exuberant April Fair.

As the fairground takes shape, downtown Sevilla becomes something of a ghost town. Businesses close down for the week, schools let out, and people prepare for a holiday across the river. All across Spain, Sevillanos catch trains to return home. The April Fair is a kind of annual family reunion. It's a time to catch up with family, reconnect with friends, and celebrate Andalusian heritage.

Though the April Fair is a family affair, casual tourists can still join in the festivities. There's no admission charge to enter the fairground. By day, you can enjoy the parades, the locals in colorful costumes, and amusement park rides. At night, it's easy to mingle with partiers who spill out into the streets. The *casetas* themselves are private, but everyone is so happy that it's not unheard of to strike up an impromptu friendship, become a "special guest," and be invited in. And a couple of tents—sponsored by the city or the Communist Party (cheers!)—are open to everyone.

The fair officially begins Monday night. People gather in their personal party tent, their *caseta*, and spend the evening socializing over food and drinks. Monday is the *noche del pescaito*—the night of fish—so the menu focuses on seafood. As midnight approaches, crowds gather around the fairground's huge arched entryway. With the TV cameras rolling, the mayor throws a switch, lighting the thousands of lightbulbs that adorn the gate. This begins a chain reaction as, one by one, the sections of the grounds get illuminated. Let the fair begin!

The fairground is crisscrossed with avenues lined with colorful lanterns and striped party tents, where people gather inside with friends and family.

An Equestrian Fashion Show

This begins six more days of festivities, with each day following a familiar ritual.

Mornings are sleepy and relaxed. Then, around noon, the promenading starts. It's a parade of horses and their well-dressed riders. Andalucía has been known for centuries for producing some of the world's finest purebred horses. The classic Andalusian steeds have gray coats (though there are many other colors), long tails, calm personalities, and good jumping ability. Dressage and the equestrian arts are huge here. Andalucía is home to a famous equestrian school (similar to the Lippizaners in Vienna), where they perform horse ballets set to Spanish music.

At the Fair, horses and riders clip-clop proudly up and down the streets. Spectators open the flaps of their *casetas* and watch from the shade. Riders sit ramrod straight, while colorfully clad señoritas ride sidesaddle. Horse carriages also parade through the streets. Some horses are nearly as dressed up as the people.

The parading tradition has been part of the Fair since it began in 1848. Back then, the festival was basically a county fair where livestock breeders showcased their animals. In keeping with the tradition, today's riders continue on to the bullring, where they meet up with other breeders.

Over the decades, the original livestock focus evolved. Just like American county fairs evolved into a celebration of traditional Americana, the April Fair celebrates Andalusian roots.

A HUMAN FASHION SHOW

The April Fair is Sevilla's social event of the year. It's hip to be square. Rich and famous celebrities and trendy hipsters don traditional costumes in a kind of urban chic. Nowhere is that clearer than in what people wear to the festival. It's a dress-up affair. The April Fair is the place to debut the latest trends in traditional Andalusian clothing.

Flamenco dresses and fans (decorative as well as practical) make a flirtatious fashion statement.

Men wear the traditional "*caballero*" outfit—short jacket and wide-brimmed hat (though nowadays, many men wear business suits-and-ties or formal wear). Remember that, in Spanish, the word for "gentleman" is the same as the word for "horseman"—*caballero*.

Women wear brightly colored flamenco dresses, with exotic patterns and ruffled hems. This is a big deal here, and local women take it very seriously. To the casual eye, the dresses may all look alike, but the styles subtly change every year. Women save up all year to have flamenco dresses custom-made for the April Fair. They're considered an important status symbol.

Women accessorize with a tasseled shawl, a tortoiseshell comb in their hair (or cheaper plastic), and a color-coordinating flower on their heads. A matching, folding fan completes the look. The fan is not merely to cool off. It's also a crucial part of flamenco dancing. And it can be used to flash coded messages in the flirtation rituals—it is spring, after all.

The Art of the Bullfight

While the horse parades go on, there's another major event just across the river— bullfights. During the April Fair, bullfights are held daily, and they always feature the season's top bulls and matadors.

Sevilla is the birthplace of bullfighting; its arena is one of the oldest and most prestigious. Because the April Fair originated among livestock breeders, bullfighting has always been a part of the scene. It's a showcase for the strongest bulls and the most skilled horses and *caballeros*.

The crowd roars as the first bull explodes out of the chute and enters the arena. Sevillanos are connoisseurs of bullfighting. They appreciate how the mounted *picadors* skillfully maneuver their horses to stab the bull and wear him down. In fact, bullfighting began (in the 1500s) as training for mounted knights in battle. As it developed, Sevilla was on the cutting edge of the various innovations: the matador's scarlet cape, the "suit of lights," and the elevation of the matador to celebrity status.

In the next phase of the bullfight, the *banderilleros* run straight at the bull, jump, and try to plant two spikes in the bull's back. Finally, the matador takes his turn. He flashes a cape to distract the bull, and stands absolutely still while the bull brushes just past his hip. The bullfight always ends the same: The matador stabs the bull with his sword, and the bull always dies.

While this strikes many people as cruel brutality, many Sevillanos consider bullfighting an art form. (Fights are covered in the culture section of the newspaper, not in the sports section.) They appreciate the nobility of the beast, excellent horsemanship, and the courage and grace of the matador. If the fight is deemed a good one, they call for one of the bull's ears to be given as a trophy to the matador. In Sevilla, matadors are rock stars.

As the birthplace of bullfighting, Sevilla hosts the sport's most prestigious events during the Fair.

As the sun sets, the bullfights end. People shuttle back across the river to the fairground. By now the easygoing horse-and-fashion parade is also winding down. In early evening (20:00), the festival's mood changes abruptly. The streets are cleared of four-footed ungulates, and bipedal party animals take over.

PARTYING 24/6

The party goes on literally 24 hours a day for the next six straight days and nights. Spaniards are known for their partying stamina. It's not unusual for entire families—adults, grandparents, and little kids—to stay up feasting, singing, and dancing until sunrise.

Frankly, it's not that much different from the rest of the year. Spaniards love to stay up late strolling the streets in the evening *paseo*. They greet their neighbors, nibble on tapas, get an ice cream for the kids, and show off their fancy new shoes while checking out everyone else's. In the heat of the summer, restaurants barely open before 10:00 p.m. Discos don't open until midnight and routinely stay open until the sun rises. So the April Fair festivities are just a concentrated version of the typical Spanish lifestyle.

What's their secret? Part of it is the siesta—the mid-afternoon downtime, which traditionally includes a meal with family and a maybe a nap. The other part is that Spaniards know how to pace themselves.

Whenever they drink, there's always food along with it. At the Fair, each *caseta* is always well-stocked with a bar and buffet at the back. They snack on tapas—that is, hors d'oeuvres speared with a toothpick or small fork, or atop a piece of bread. Sevillanos love fried calamari, prawns, and octopus (especially on that first "seafood" Monday). There's traditional gazpacho (zesty cold tomato soup), scrambled eggs (*revueltos*), or oxtail stew. And of course, there are plenty of desserts, like churros, dipped in hot pudding-like chocolate.

The most treasured delicacy is *jamón*—cured ham that's sliced thin and served

cold. Like connoisseurs of fine wine, Spaniards debate the merits of different breeds of pigs, what part of the pig they're eating, what the pig has eaten, and the quality of curing. Spanish bars proudly hang ham hocks from their ceilings as part of their decor.

The classic drink at the April Fair is sherry. Sherry is a fortified wine made from different vintages that are mixed together and aged in an elaborate stack of

oak barrels. The result is not the sweet dessert sherry common in the States. It's dry *fino* sherry (or its local cousin, *manzanilla*), served chilled, along with tapas. There's also a lighter drink called *rebujito*—a sherry spritz mixed with a 7 Up-type soda.

By midnight, the *fino* is flowing freely and the *casetas* are rocking. Partiers spill out into the streets.

Music is everywhere. Most *casetas* have their own soundtrack, whether a stereo, a live band, or just a friend who plays guitar. Flamenco guitarists, with their lightning-fast finger-roll strums, are among the best in the world. Flamenco is centuries-old, and in the raspy-voiced singers, you'll hear echoes of the Muslim call to prayer.

Everybody gets into it. Flamenco is a happening, with people taking turns dancing. Bystanders clap along, play castanets, and cheer on the dancers with whoops and shouts. At April Fair time, they always play certain songs everyone knows, from grandmas to kiddies. These are "the Sevillanas"—the most traditional of Andalusian folk dances. The guitar and palm-clapping set a fiery beat. But unlike the machine-gun heel stomps of most flamenco, the Sevillanas steps are graceful and simple. Dancers pose with hands on hips and one foot slightly raised. Then take a few steps forward and backward. They raise their arms above their head and turn their hands in graceful castanet-turning motions. Then, gracefully turn around and repeat. As the music stirs them, suddenly mom and dad are taking a turn at it, rekindling their romance. Meanwhile, grandma is teaching the steps to the five-year-olds.

The all-night parties wind down as sunrise leaks through the flaps of the *casetas*. Partiers sleep in. They also know they can catch a little siesta later. By noon, the next parade of horses, carriages, *caballeros*, and señoritas begins, and the April Fair ritual starts up again.

A Fair to Remember

For seven days and six nights, the April Fair attends to its rituals of horses, bullfights, tapas, sherry, and dancing late into the night. An estimated 5 million people do some version of this at the Fair during the week.

It all builds up to the weekend nights, when more than 800,000 people are packed into the fairground. There are locals in their *casetas* and strolling tourists.

Parents take their kids on the carnival rides or to see a live concert. Everyone is enjoying the party as it spills out into the streets.

Families have used this past week to reconnect. Wives have gotten to know their in-laws better, and grandpas bond with their grandkids. People catch up with their old co-workers, school chums, and football amigos. They enjoy their version of "home cooking," of local tapas and special wines and sherries. Young

software engineers and HR managers who now work in far-off Madrid remember where they came from. They've put on their traditional clothes, sung together, and danced the Sevillanas.

As the Fair reaches its close, the skies are lit up with a dazzling fireworks show, a tradition that dates back 150 years. For the kids, the whole scene creates lifelong memories that will be replayed in the next generation.

THE PALIO IN SIENA

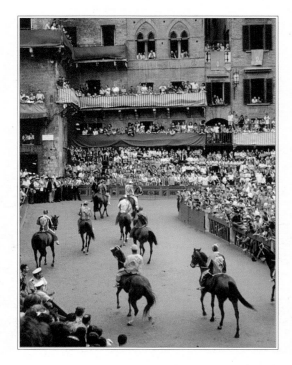

SIENA—MEDIEVAL AND MODERN

Siena is one of the best-preserved medieval cities in Europe, and, centuries later, the Sienese keep the vibrant medieval spirit alive with a festival called the Palio. They celebrate traditions that have been passed down for centuries in settings that still look like they did in the Middle Ages. This isn't some hokey chamber-of-commerce tourist event. It's bred into the bone of every Sienese citizen from birth.

To celebrate the Palio, the Sienese dress up in medieval garb and parade through the streets, drumming and waving flags. They worship together at the cathedral. They gather with friends and family for lavish community banquets. And it all culminates in the event that has brought the city its international fame—the crazy horse race called the Palio. The Palio is held twice a year, on July

The medieval ambience of Siena is the perfect setting for the medieval-era festival called the Palio.

2 and August 16. Each time it's a four-day festival capped by a frenzied horse race that decides which neighborhood is the victor.

IL CAMPO—THE HEART OF SIENA

The center of the festivities is the magnificent main square in the middle of Siena known as Il Campo. The piazza is arguably the best in all Italy—and that's saying something.

This will serve as the theater for the dramatic spectacle of the horse race. The backdrop is the massive City Hall, with its soaring tower. From there, the brick-paved square fans out, almost like an amphitheater. All around, the square is enclosed by a curving arc of harmonious red-brown palaces, creating an elegant shell-shaped space.

Il Campo is the heart of Siena—both geographically and metaphorically. It's the city's gathering place. Friends text each other and say "Meet you there in ten." They chat over a leisurely coffee or glass of Brunello at one of the surrounding cafés.

The square is the historic junction of Siena's 17 traditional neighborhoods. As we'll see, these neighborhoods, called *contrade*, are fiercely competitive. But at Il

Siena's vast main piazza, before and during the Palio.

Campo, everyone can meet and put their guard down—it's considered neutral territory, the place where everyone is simply a citizen of Siena.

Il Campo still looks like it did 700 years ago, during Siena's golden age, when it first hosted the Palio horse race. Back then, Il Campo was a bustling marketplace, selling goods to European travelers as they passed through along the main north-south highway to Rome. Siena's wool merchants needed money-changers, which led the Sienese to virtually invent a new occupation—banking.

By 1300, with a population of 50,000, Siena was as big as Paris. The City Hall was a proud symbol of self-government—the Palazzo Pubblico, or Palace of the People. Its skyscraping tower stood like a 330-foot declaration of independence from kings, emperors, and popes. There was a public fountain on the square—the artfully decorated Fountain of Joy—to bring fresh water (and joy) to ordinary citizens. By the mid-1300s, Siena was even on track to build the largest cathedral the world had ever seen.

But then came the disaster known to Europe as the Black Death of 1348—the bubonic plague. In 1348, Siena was a wealthy city of 70,000 people. Two years

Il Campo's towering City Hall and playful Fountain of Joy reflect the glory of Siena's golden age in the 1300s.

later, it had dropped to 45,000. The economy tanked, Florence got the upper hand, and Siena humbly faded into the background of history.

But Siena's loss became our sightseeing gain. Because the city was too poor to rebuild, they ended up pickled in a medieval brine. The city slumbered for several centuries, and old traditions continued on, unchanged.

Today, Siena is a delightful mix of that centuries-old medieval ambience and modern energy. It's a city of 50,000 bankers and merchants living happily within historic buildings. The pedestrian-friendly streets are lined with trendy fashion boutiques and elegant restaurants. In the evening, strolling locals spill out into the streets to grab an ice cream to-go and make the scene on their *passeggiata*. Many consider Siena to be Italy's ultimate Tuscan hill town.

At Palio time, you feel both the old tradition and modern energy. That's when bankers, I.T. specialists, and internationally-renowned chefs shed their modern garb and return to their neighborhood roots. The *contrade* get into it as much now as they did centuries ago. And on the day of the big race—when you're packed onto Il Campo with 60,000 people—believe me, you'll feel it: The heart of medieval Siena still beats strong.

THE *CONTRADE*— CENTURIES-OLD RIVALRIES RESURFACE

The Palio is much more than a few days in July and August. All year long, citizens prepare for the summer ahead. Women lovingly stitch medieval-style vests and colorful banners. Neighborhood fathers coach kids in the traditional arts of drumming and flag throwing.

All of this activity centers around the neighborhood, or *contrada*. Each of the city's 17 traditional neighborhoods is a self-contained world, with its own parish church and a square where people gather. Traditionally, each *contrada* had a specialty trade, such as the neighborhood of shoemakers.

Each *contrada* has its unique colors and its unique mascot. For example, the "Owl" neighborhood has a local coat of arms with an owl emblazoned on a background of red and black pyramids. Most of these totemic mascots are fierce animals, like eagle, dragon, and wolf. Others are cute: turtle, porcupine, and snail. Still others represent primeval forces of nature, like forest and wave. These insignia are posted as small signs on street corners, marking the boundaries of each neighborhood. Besides that, for much of the year, the *contrade* and their emblems are pretty low-key.

But as the Palio approaches, the battle lines are drawn. The "gang colors" come out. The streets get lined with the distinctive flags of each *contrada*. Residents break out their bandanas with their colors and tie them around their necks. They put on T-shirts emblazoned with their mascot and patterns. They start trash-talking with their friends about whose neighborhood is best, and who'll win the big race. There are office pools, and bets are placed. Centuries-old rivalries are suddenly alive again.

It's Palio time.

Each neighborhood (or contrada) has its own coat of arms with distinct colors and a totemic emblem.

Horses and Jockeys, Flag-Throwing, and Marching

The first big event is the much-anticipated lottery, when the competing *contrade* and horses are selected. Of the 17 neighborhoods, only 10 can be chosen for the race. That leaves seven neighborhoods broken-hearted and watching from the sidelines. Another lottery assigns which horse will compete for each *contrada*. They hire jockeys. It's so competitive that they often bring in professionals.

But it's the horses that are the stars. Once their horse is assigned to them (even though it's random), the *contrada* embraces the animal as a member of their community. The horse is showered with love and respect. They groom it and wash it and pamper it, and keep it in a four-star stable right in the city center. Everyone in the neighborhood wants to see their four-legged champion, so they take it out and walk it through the streets to show it off to the admiring fans.

Each competing contrada *has its own horse, which becomes a beloved family member.*

Festivities are punctuated by medieval flag-waving and flag-throwing demonstrations. Young men practice for it all year long.

In the weeks leading up to the race, *contrada* pride erupts in countless ways. If you're ever in Siena and hear the thunder of distant drumming, head for it. There's a good chance it's a *contrada* on parade.

The parade winds through the narrow lanes. In the front are men dressed in colorful tights and medieval doublets, with the neighborhood colors and patterns. With pomp and pageantry, drummers set the beat. Others carry long rectangular banners on a pole with the neighborhood insignia. Still others carry big flags with the *contrada* symbols. These are the flag-throwers, carrying on a medieval tradition. They swish the flags back and forth. They jump over each other's flags. They twirl them like majorettes, then toss them in the air, and catch them again. They've trained for this all year. To drop the flag now would bring dishonor to their neighborhood. With the waving flags and pounding drums, it all harkens back to Middle Ages when these rituals boosted morale before battle.

Regular Sienese add the modern touch. They march alongside, dressed in casual clothes and a bandana. As they march, they belt out passionate team songs and good-luck choruses: We're the best!

If you happen upon one of these parades in Siena, you could duck into a souvenir store, buy a scarf in *contrada* colors—and join the crowd.

Cathedral Visit—Praying for Victory

The most important of the parades is when the entire city makes its way up the hill to Siena's cathedral, or Duomo. If Il Campo is the city's secular heart, the Duomo is its soul. For 800 years, the Duomo and its 250-foot belltower—perched atop Siena's highest point—has been a beacon for pilgrims.

The various *contrade* wave their banners as they converge on the cathedral. They file through the Duomo's colorful facade of white stone, black stripes, and ornaments of green, white, pink, and gold. They enter the nave, with its forest of zebra-striped columns and colorful inlaid-marble floors.

They're surrounded everywhere by reminders of Siena's greatness. The she-wolf statue recalls Siena's legendary origins as a cousin of Rome. The rose window by the artist Duccio speaks to Siena's role in jump-starting the Renaissance. Two

The various contrade *parade into Siena's cathedral.*

wooden flagpoles are a constant reminder of the crucial battle 700 years ago when Siena defeated Florence, ushering in their golden age.

Finally, there's the venerable painting of the Virgin Mary called the Madonna del Voto. For eight centuries, Sienese citizens have knelt before this icon and asked Mary for her help. At Palio time, each of the *contrade* make their way here to pray for victory. And whoever wins will return here jubilantly afterward to thank the Madonna by leaving a small offering. Today, the church walls are adorned with such offerings from grateful worshippers and winning *contrade*.

Once inside, the parade of *contrade* take their places on either side of the nave. They wave their neighborhood banners.

But the centerpiece of the parade is one special banner. This banner, or *palio*, is the trophy given to the winner of the horse race, and what gives the "Palio di Siena" its name. There's a new banner made every year, by a local artist. Each year's

The priest blesses the palio—the Virgin Mary banner which will be awarded to the winner.

artist is given artistic license, but must include a few time-honored symbols, like coats of arms and symbols of the city. Most important—at the top, and most visible of all—there's always an image of the Virgin Mary. Mary is much adored in Siena. The city, the cathedral, and the Palio are all dedicated to her. Even the dates of the races relate to Mary: The July 2 race celebrates miracles attributed to a Sienese icon of Mary, and August 16 honors the Assumption of Mary.

The *palio* banner is brought into the church and is slowly paraded up the nave. As it passes, the *contrade* wave their stirring flags in unison. The *palio* reaches the altar, where the priest is ready for the solemn occasion—the blessing of the *palio*. The priest says a few words, sprinkles holy water, and blesses the banner. Now blessed, it will soon be awarded to the victorious *contrada*.

THE PRE-RACE BANQUET— SAME MENU SINCE DUCCIO ATE HERE

Before the big race, the Sienese gather in their neighborhood square for a big, communal banquet. It starts early in the evening and continues long into the warm summer night. They feast on Tuscan delicacies and hearty sangiovese wine. They finish the meal by dunking *cantucci*—biscotti with almonds baked in—into their local dessert wine, or *vin santo*. Invented in Siena, these biscotti are now found in coffee shops worldwide.

It's at these pre-race banquets that it becomes crystal clear how deeply rooted the Palio is in the Sienese psyche. It's a scene that has changed little over the centuries, and the walls echo with time-honored pageantry and ritual. Between courses, there are rousing choruses proclaiming their *contrada*'s greatness. They stand together and sing the *contrada* hymn, leaving many people deeply moved. The emotion is contagious and the wine is delightful.

The banquet is a multigenerational affair. Many attendees are gearing up for their 100th Palio—that's two a year for 50 years. They share the table with the

young, while the very young turn somersaults by the fountain, soaking up the centuries-old traditions. In a few decades, these kids will be attending a very similar banquet, in the same place, eating the same foods, and passing it on to their kids and grandkids.

For the Sienese, the Palio is not just a festival—it's a way of life. Locals joke about their fate: "If you're Sienese," they say, "you're born, there's the Palio—and then you die."

PREPARING THE SQUARE

As the big day approaches, Il Campo is transformed into a race track. Construction workers assemble bleacher seats around the perimeter. They haul in tons of clay and pack it down to make the track. Railings are erected around the center of the square, where more spectators will gather. Mattress-type padding is put up

at the sharpest corners to protect the walls and buildings—and the horses and riders, who often crash. No matter what the workers do, they can't hide the fact that it's still an unbelievably weird place for a horse race. Il Campo is small, tilted, and shell-shaped, with lots of odd angles. But it's how they've done it since the races began, and always will.

The day before the race, there are a couple of warm-up events in the square. There's the "Charge of the Carabinieri," where men dressed up as cavalry soldiers ride in on horseback in their plumed hats and sabers. They trot around the track a few times, build up a little speed, race once around the track . . . and then exit the square while the crowd applauds. There's also a practice run with the actual horses and jockeys. This gives the jockeys a chance to get to know their horses (and vice versa), and to get used to the track. They don't go full speed, but it's still pretty thrilling, and only serves to whet the Sienese appetite for the real thing.

The city is wound tight. Over the weeks, the anticipation has built: The horses have been selected in a nerve-wracking lottery. They've been trained and pampered. The *contrade* have paraded, boasting of their centuries-old prowess. Jockeys have been hired, bets placed, trash talked. Now the big day has arrived.

Bleachers are set up and workers clean the main square to get ready for race day.

On race day, the full range of Palio pageantry has to repeat itself one last time. The time-honored rituals begin early in the morning, in the city's cafés, where locals, police, and security personnel fuel up with their morning jolt of cappuccino. Then those honored to represent their *contrada* dress up in medieval costumes and sweltering suits of armor. This requires many assistants who not only help fit the clothing but make sure it looks just as it did 500 years ago.

In full regalia, the *contrade* then parade to their neighborhood church. There they wow their friends and family with an elaborate flag-twirling and flag-throwing ceremony, to the rhythm of the drums. This is followed by a full-throated singing of the *contrada's* hymn.

Finally, the beloved horse is led in. It stands facing the assembled crowd. The parish priest steps up, waves his arms, and gives the horse a pre-race blessing. "Now go," says the priest to the beast: "Go and return victorious."

Then—you guessed it—there's yet another procession. With drums pounding and flags flying, each *contrada* leaves their neighborhood church and marches one

Even before the race itself, there's much spectacle on Il Campo. Then on race day everyone packs the square, the jockeys maneuver their horses to the starting line, and . . .

more time up to the cathedral. There they do another flag-throwing demonstration for the bishop, showcasing their talents and passion before all Siena.

As race time approaches, all of the *contrade* start heading downhill in one last grand parade through the canyon-like streets. With drums thundering, locals and tourists alike crush to join the scene. Everyone converges on the center of Siena, where it all goes down—Il Campo.

THE RACE

… and they're off! Horses careen and jockeys tumble, until one horse crosses the finish line, and…

It's nearly time for the race. The square is already pretty full, as crowds have been arriving since the crack of dawn. Some splurge for the reserved bleacher seats. In the surrounding apartments, the owners welcome friends to watch from the best

spot in town—the balconies. Everyone else packs into the center, where it's free admission but standing-room only. By evening, Il Campo is stuffed to the brim with 60,000 fans—that's more than the entire population of the city. Standing shoulder to shoulder, they're sweating and partying, with noisemakers, neighborhood scarves, and straining bladders. (How do they do it? Depends.)

The centuries-old ritual begins as a cart pulled by oxen enters the square, carrying the *palio* banner. At its sight, the crowd goes wild. They anxiously anticipate taking the coveted trophy home to their *contrada*.

Then the horses are led in: ten snorting horses and their very nervous riders. They approach the starting line, behind a rope stretched across the track. It takes a while as the horses prance and the jockeying includes a little last-minute negotiating. The horses line up, the crowd is hushed. For a moment, there's silence.

...and the winning neighborhood goes berserk.

Then . . .

 . . . they're off!

As the crowd roars, the horses sprint away like crazy, heading clockwise around the square. The jockeys play bumper cars. There's only one rule: There are no rules. Horses skid and tumble. Jockeys, forced to ride bareback, hang on for dear life, and many bite the dust. The horses go once around the square—about 400 yards. Then once again. After the third lap, the crowd cheers madly, waving their scarves as they approach the finish. The horses streak across the finish line.

The crowd goes berserk. Or rather, one-seventeenth of Siena—the winning *contrada*—goes berserk. Tears of joy flow, people embrace. The losers (figuratively) writhe and gnash their teeth in agony. For the winning *contrada*, the jubilation is over the top. Even some losing *contrade* enjoy a delicious dose of schadenfreude if their arch-enemy *contrada* lost badly.

After months of preparation, parading, and pageantry, that's it—it's all over. The whole thing took barely 90 seconds.

The happy horde pours out of Il Campo and thunders through the streets back up to the cathedral. Once there, they pack the church. They give thanks to the Virgin Mary for their victory, in a ritual that's gone on here virtually every year since medieval times. Then, in a solemn-but-joyous ceremony, the winning *contrada* is awarded their prize. It's not money or a big gold trophy—just that simple banner, the coveted *palio*. But the winning neighborhood has also won something even more precious—bragging rights to call themselves champions . . . at least until the next race.

THE RUNNING OF THE BULLS
IN PAMPLONA

PAMPLONA—
HOST FOR A ONE-OF-A-KIND SPECTACLE

THE RUNNING OF THE BULLS is one of Europe's most exuberant festivals and craziest spectacles. Each July, throngs of red-and-white-clad visitors descend on the city to watch bullfights, drink sangria, and purposely place themselves in a life-or-death situation: racing with a stampeding herd of angry bulls. It all takes place in Pamplona, in northern Spain, a city of stout old walls standing guard in the foothills of the Pyrenees. Many locals speak Basque and call the town by its Basque name—"Iruña." It's a city of 200,000 people that's both traditional (with a charming Old Town of narrow lanes) and affluent (with a sleek new infrastructure). In July, the population balloons to a million, enjoying nine days of carousing, music, parades, and fireworks.

The festival's starring attraction repeats itself every morning, when bulls are herded at top speed through the center of town. Brave and foolhardy revelers

This crazy festival has been immortalized by Ernest Hemingway, by this statue, and by the stories of bull runners who lived to run again.

try to run ahead of the thundering bulls without getting killed. Thousands come here to prove their manhood, while tens of thousands of others line the streets to watch them succeed . . . or get trampled and gored. It's a one-of-a-kind event, transmitted live via TV all over Spain to a riveted audience of millions.

A MASH-UP OF PIETY AND LIVESTOCK

Ironically, this crazy time of drinking, danger, and debauchery starts out with . . . a church service.

The Running of the Bulls is officially known as the Festival of San Fermín, and the celebration is built around the city's patron saint. Two thousand years ago, Saint Fermín was an outspoken Christian living in a pagan Roman city. It had been founded by Julius Caesar's son-in-law, Pompey—hence the town's name of "Pomp"-lona. Fermín was arrested for his faith and decapitated. But his memory lived on. The date of his martyrdom became a day of special Masses, religious processions, feasts, and general revelry.

And so it is that on the morning of July 6—the first day of the festival—Pamplonans gather at the Chapel of San Fermín. It's a capacity crowd that includes the city council and other VIPs. There's no question what to wear for this Mass: red, which symbolizes the blood spilled in Fermín's martyrdom.

They honor a venerable 500-year-old silver statue of Saint Fermín. The statue is also a reliquary. If you squint, you can see that, just below his Adam's apple, there's a receptacle holding Fermín's actual finger. This relic has been venerated for centuries by pilgrims passing through as they walk from France to Spain on the Camino de Santiago pilgrimage route. Even today, thousands of modern pilgrims hike through Pamplona, following yellow arrows pointing the way.

For the festival, the statue of Fermín is dressed up in red robes and a golden bishop's hat. It will be paraded around town, to be adored by thousands. This is just the first of many parades and celebrations over the days to follow.

Over the centuries, the Festival of San Fermín grew. The saint's feast day happened to coincide with the time of year when local livestock breeders herded their bulls from their pen (at one end of town) to the bullring (on the other end). This event, called El Encierro ("The Enclosing"), became a nickname for the festival still used today. Over the years, brave young men took the occasion to show off their athleticism and expertise with bulls by running alongside them. Occasionally some got injured. Onlookers gathered.

A festival was born.

IF BULLS WERE TOURISTS

The bull-running part of the festival begins at City Hall at noon, after the morning church service. Dignitaries step onto the flag-bedecked balcony of the building's Baroque facade, with its macho Hercules statue, lions, and a horn-blower trumpeting Pamplona's greatness. As the mayor proclaims the start of the festival, the crowd cheers.

For the next nine days, the City Hall (Ayuntamiento) will be ground zero for

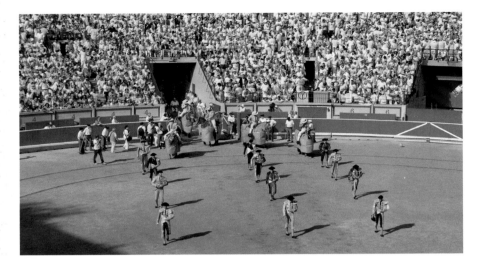

this sprawling festival. It serves as the starting line for the daily running of the bulls.

The Running of the Bulls route runs right through the center of Pamplona's Old Town, or Casco Antiguo. If the bulls were tourists, they'd get a good look at Pamplona's major sights. From City Hall, they head down La Estafeta street, home to the city's most fun shops and liveliest tapas bars. They pass a street-corner shrine to San Fermín, and a café where hungry locals dunk churros into molten chocolate. There's the colorful food market, featuring the regional sheep-milk cheeses, and the hole-in-the-wall Beatriz shop with Pamplona's best mini-croissants. Continuing on, the route skirts right along the edge of the city's large main square, Plaza del Castillo.

Finally the bulls will reach their "finish line"—the Plaza de Toros. Pamplona's bullfighting arena is the third-biggest in the world, after Madrid and Mexico City. It's used only nine days out of the year, exclusively for the festival. Tickets are very expensive and are sold out every day. Here the bulls that run in the morning will fulfill their purpose in life—when they meet their matador in a bullfight.

Bullfighting, though considered cruel by many, is honored here as a primeval contest. The bull is respected as a symbol of power, life, and the great wild. "Bullfighting is the only art in which the artist is in danger of death," said the author who put Pamplona on the map—Ernest Hemingway.

The Sun Also Rises

The American literary giant Ernest Hemingway is celebrated by Pamplona as if he were a native son. There's a statue of him at the end of the Running of the Bulls route. At the beginning of each festival, young people tie a red neckerchief around his statue so he can be properly outfitted for the occasion.

Hemingway came here for the first time for the 1923 festival. Inspired by the spectacle, he wrote his classic *The Sun Also Rises.* The novel crystallized the allure of this festival: an exotic locale where restless bohemians come in search of themselves. They drink and carouse, find romance, and test their bravery against fierce bulls. That adventurous image ricocheted across the literary world, and made the festival instantly famous.

People poured in to follow in Hemingway's footsteps. Even today, visitors can

American writer Ernest Hemingway put Pamplona (and bullfighting) on the cultural map. His fans flock to Café Iruña, one of many places he frequented.

see Hemingway's favorite hotel (Gran Hotel La Perla), with his original furniture. There's the Bar Txoko and Café Iruña where Hemingway drank (among many other places in town).

When Hemingway first visited, Pamplona was a dusty town of 30,000 with an obscure bullfighting festival. When he returned for the last time in 1959, it had gotten so out of hand that he reportedly regretted popularizing it.

But after its growing pains, the festival has settled down to become more adult and sophisticated. Despite all the alcohol, things feel in control and reasonably sane. Now, a million people a year come here for a touch of the primeval. As Hemingway himself put it, he enjoyed seeing wild animals running together: one on four legs, and the other on two.

By day, there are parades of giant mannequins.

Parades, Sangria, and All-Night Dancing in the Streets

The festival kicks into high gear. It's nine full days and nights of nonstop action.

Each day brings a different parade. People carry towering *gegantes*—huge mannequins popular in northern Spain. These might depict medieval kings and saints dear to the town, or just regional celebrities, all adding a playful mystique to the festivities. There are plenty of fun activities for the kids. Live music is everywhere, set up in many different venues. After dark, the Old Town becomes one big open-air party. On the main square, the venerable Café Iruña pulses with music and dance.

At night, the whole town is one big party—in bars and elegant cafés, sleeping it off on the sidewalks, and dancing in the streets 'til dawn.

To beat the heat, participants chug the festival's most iconic drink—*kalimotxo* (in Basque, or *calimocho* in Spanish). This is a special sangria made of half red wine, half cola.

The whole town is caught up in the spirit—the masses fill the streets, while VIPs fill the city's venerable ballrooms. Fireworks light up the sultry night sky. Partiers fuel themselves with alcoholic courage to face tomorrow's big challenge, when they'll run with the bulls. The festival's energy courses through the city. When you're out dancing in the streets at 4:00 in the morning with a sangria-charged mob, it's hard to visualize that, in just a few hours, this same street will be hosting a very different spectacle—the Running of the Bulls.

No Bull—This is Serious Business

"Do not touch the wounded," booms the voice on the loudspeaker. "That is the responsibility of the health personnel."

As day dawns, this announcement echoes through the streets of Pamplona. The cleaning crew is clearing away last night's garbage and broken glass. A line of green-fluorescent-vested policemen rouses passed-out drunks. They question would-be bull-runners to see if they're up to the task. You can't be too intoxicated, or wear flimsy sandals, or carry a backpack that could distract the bulls.

The bull-running route is readied: Medics staff their stations, workers pick up last night's party trash, and police make sure runners are up for the task.

The streets along the route are readied for the onslaught of rampaging bulls and revelers. Shop windows are boarded up, and fencing erected to keep the bulls on course and protect the crowd and buildings. In important spots there's a double barrier, with a space in between for the journalists and the all-important first-responders. TV cameras are put up everywhere to catch every possible injury—on cranes, with robotic arms run by remote control, and vice-gripped to windowsills. The street—just hours ago filled with throngs of all-night revelers—is now sanitized for a televised spectacle.

The Running of the Bulls takes place every morning at 8:00, but the crowds start massing long before that. (Too early in the morning? For some revelers, it's still last night.) Spectators claim a good viewing spot along the barriers, until it's a wall of bodies.

In front of City Hall, the street starts to fill with runners. Most are dressed in the traditional outfit: white pants and shirt, with a red bandana tied around their neck and another around their waist. One legend says it's to honor Saint Fermín (white for purity) who was martyred (red for blood). Another says it's the dress of butchers, who supposedly began the tradition. Which legend is true? Frankly, the bulls are color-blind and the runners are blind-drunk, and no one really cares.

Everyone's attention is focused on the starting point, where restless bulls rustle in their pens.

There are two distinct classes of runners: *mozos* and bozos.

The vast majority are clueless out-of-towners and frat boys, just here for the thrill. Their courage stoked by booze and the girls they're trying to impress, most are just finishing up a night of drinking.

The serious runners are Pamplonans called *mozos*. They respect the ritual, train for the event, and run every year. They're local celebrities, known for their courage and expertise. They've surveyed the bulls' photos and stats, printed in yesterday's paper, and studied their quirks. While other runners are hung over (at best), the *mozos* have gotten a good night's sleep, and are now stretching and focusing.

The *mozos* have a plan. You might think it's best to get a good head start and just try to outrun the bulls. Many amateurs do exactly that. But the *mozos* actively court danger. This is to show off their skill and knowledge of the bulls, like how a matador purposely tries to get as close to the bull as he can. So, rather than run the whole half-mile route, *mozos* pick a short stretch of it for their close encounter. They know where the street slants uphill, where the sharp turns and odd corners are, and where they can escape behind the barriers. They know that if they fall, they shouldn't try to get up—it's better to be trampled by six bulls than to be gored by one.

The ideal "run" is to stay just in front of the bull's nose, for as long as possible— usually just a few seconds—before diving out of the way. It's like surfing: You hope to catch a good wave and ride it as long as you can until it's passed. What's the mark of a truly gnarly run? They say it's when you can feel the breath of the bull on the back of your legs.

The Bulls are Loose

As 8:00 approaches, the energy surges. The area around City Hall is so packed with runners, if everyone suddenly stampeded at once, it'd be deadly. Onlookers

And they're off! The bulls charge and runners scramble.

line the barricades and fill the side alleys. The bulls are penned up tightly a block away, ready to explode. The *mozos* begin jockeying for a good starting spot.

The anxious runners sing the traditional song, pleading to San Fermín for divine help: *A San Fermín pedimos, por ser nuestro patrón, nos guíe en el encierro, dándonos su bendición.* "We ask Saint Fermín, because he is our patron, to guide us through the Running of the Bulls, giving us his blessing."

The clock atop City Hall inches its hand toward eight. The seconds tick down, until . . .

At 8:00, a rocket is fired—the bulls have been set loose! Moments later a second rocket means the last of the bulls has left the pen.

The adrenaline surges in the crowded street. Everyone wants to start running—but not too early, lest you show how scared you are. Like a thousand pogo sticks, a sea of runners begins jumping up and down, craning to see exactly where the rampaging bulls are, to time their flight. The bulls come into view.

Then the runners run like hell.

Six big bulls come roaring down the street. Each one is a thundering mass of 2,000-pound fury. They will be stampeded a total of a half-mile through the town—from their pens to the bullfighting arena—kept on course by the fencing alongside. Because a bull is most dangerous when it breaks free from the pack,

Some runners find safety along the walls. Others are not so lucky.

they're herded along by a few steers, whose calmer presence helps keep the bulls together. Experienced *mozos* know their steers from their bulls. There's no greater embarrassment in this *muy* macho culture than to boast that you've run with a bull, only to be told he was actually a "bull" that's been castrated.

The first stretch is uphill, allowing the bulls to use their strong hind legs to pick up speed. When they reach the top of La Estafeta street and make the turn, it's one of the most hair-raising points on the course. Here, the bulls are now going downhill, and often lose their balance and start sliding into the barricades. They regain their footing and charge down La Estafeta. The street is very narrow: No room for barricades . . . no escape for daredevils.

The animals race down the street. It's a red-and-white cauldron of desperation: big eyes, scrambling bodies, the ground quaking. Panicky frat boys press against the fences, making themselves as flat as possible. The *mozos* allow the bulls to come close. Then they try to run just in front of them for as long as they can, before diving out of the way at the last second. Some duck into the openings in the fencing just big enough for a skinny *mozo* to escape.

Cruel as this all seems for the bulls—who scramble for footing on the cobblestones as they rush toward their doom in the bullring—it's the humans that take the brunt of it. Runners fall and are trampled by bulls or their fellow runners.

After the race, runners can buy photos of their exploits. They gather in bars to watch the race on TV reruns and embellish their stories.

Others are gored by the panicky bulls. First responders leap out from behind the barricades and go to work. Dozens of people are gored, trampled, or otherwise injured. Ambulances are standing by to rush them to the ER. Over the years, 15 runners have even died. (On the other hand, Pamplona's hospital sees more people every year for alcohol-related accidents.)

The bulls rumble by, the runners scramble, the crowd cheers and gasps, and a thousand pictures are taken.

And then it's over. The bulls are gone. They've covered the entire half-mile course to the bullring in barely over two minutes.

After the Run: Reruns

The survivors pick themselves up and assess the damage. Immediately, the authorities start taking down the timber fences and stacking them for tomorrow. People fill the streets. Boarded-up shops open for business again. Photographers who've filmed the race quickly make prints to sell to runners. As is the ritual, the runners drop into a bar immediately afterward to have breakfast. There, they meet up with their friends and trade war stories about how they narrowly escaped death. They proudly show off their skinned knees and ripped clothes.

Every bar has the TV on, where the runners watch the rerun of the entire spectacle on TV—all 131 seconds of it. All day long, local channels will replay the morning's spectacle. They show highlights from every conceivable angle, in slow-mo and freeze-frame, catching every slick escape, every trampling, every spill and thrill. Famous *mozos* are interviewed to break down the intricacies of their run. And, with the routine mundane demeanor of a TV weatherman, a nurse with a clipboard comes on to announce that day's wounded.

The Running of the Bulls is over, but the festival goes on. There's another day of parades, another night of dancing in the streets, and another run tomorrow morning at 8:00 sharp. It won't be over until midnight on July 14. That's when everyone will congregate in front of City Hall as the dignitaries appear once again on the balcony to announce the end of the festival. They'll light candles, and sing their sad song, *Pobre de Mí*: "Poor me, the Fiesta de San Fermín has ended."

But for now, the runners have their own agenda. Some will spend the day at another parade or concert. Some have already hit the bars and are downing another sangria. But most are trudging back to their hotel rooms. Soon, the hallways will be lined with little plastic signs on the doorknobs: "Do Not Disturb."

BASTILLE DAY IN PARIS

BASTILLE DAY—A BEACON OF FREEDOM

EVERY NATIONALITY HAS its national holiday, its "Fourth of July," that marks its birth as a nation. Perhaps the most famous of these is in France, on July 14—Bastille Day. That's the day they celebrate the symbolic start of the French Revolution that brought down the monarchy and created modern France. The Revolution also touched off a spirt of revolution worldwide, so Bastille Day has become a touchstone for lovers of liberty everywhere. The day certainly involves a show of national patriotism, of course—waving flags, military parades, and solemn remembrances. But even more so, it's a time of wild parties. People dance in the streets, and enjoy firework displays, great food, and too much wine. Bastille Day celebrates the sheer joy of personal liberty.

LEFT: *Paris is the hub of French pride on the nation's "Independence Day."*

OPPOSITE: *Today's Parisians love the day. Louis XVI, not so much.*

THE STORMING OF THE BASTILLE— THEN AND NOW

The celebrations begin the night before, on July 13, with a huge open-air block party located on the spot where it all began—the Bastille.

Tens of thousands mob the vast 350,000-square-foot intersection called Place de la Bastille. Normally, this is a busy roundabout where several streets meet, and cars circle. But on this night it's taken over by "the people." Music blares, the surrounding cafés are jammed, partiers roam with drinks in hand, and strangers break into impromptu dancing.

The chaotic scene is vaguely similar to the mobs that swarmed here two centuries ago. That was the day when the world's history turned.

It's July of 1789. France is under the tyranny of its king, bishops, and nobles. The people are starving, thanks to the monarchy's corruption and war. In the streets of Paris, there's a new power faction rising up and demanding change—the people, who form the National Assembly.

But King Louis XVI—studious, shy, aloof, and indecisive—pushes back. He dissolves the Assembly and orders his troops to fire on innocent protestors.

The French people had had enough. Revolutionaries filled the streets of Paris.

The king's troops retreated and hunkered down inside a huge castle-like fortress. With its eight towers and 100-foot-high walls, it dominated the Parisian skyline, and had become the very symbol of oppression—the Bastille.

On the hot, muggy morning of July 14, a mob of angry citizens began massing around the Bastille's main gate. They demanded that the king's troops surrender and release the political prisoners inside. The soldiers refused. Two citizens scaled the huge wall. They cut the chains of the drawbridge—crash! The bridge came down, and the mob poured through. Terrified soldiers opened fire. Dozens were killed on both sides and hundreds wounded. At the peak of the battle, more of the king's soldiers appeared on the horizon. It looked like the fledgling Revolution was doomed.

But the new troops unexpectedly joined sides with the citizens! A loud cheer went up as they pointed their cannons at the Bastille. Finally, the soldiers in the

Bastille had no choice but to surrender. The Revolutionaries opened the dark dungeons, and brought the prisoners into the light of day. Then they paraded victoriously through Paris. On the way, they stormed City Hall (Hôtel de Ville) and arrested the king's mayor. He was literally torn apart by the hysterical crowd. His head was stuck on a stick and carried through the city. The Revolution had begun.

Today, those events of July 14, known collectively as the Storming of the Bastille, are celebrated every Bastille Day with equally colorful festivities.

Virtually no trace of the original Bastille remains on today's Place de la Bastille. The Revolutionaries dismantled the hated symbol brick by brick. But the spirit of Revolution lives on in the square. There's a 150-foot column in the middle topped with a gilded statue of Liberty symbolizing France's ongoing struggle for democracy. The French had to fight tyrants once again in the 1830 "July Revolution" and in 1848 (the struggle immortalized in *Les Misérables*). More recently, the square has hosted worker protests and the French Resistance of World War II.

Today, Place de la Bastille is a snapshot of France's open society. It's surrounded by literary cafés, multiethnic neighborhoods, and the vigor of youth. Winged Liberty carries the torch of optimism into the future.

And so Parisians still return to Place de la Bastille to remember where it all started. Exuberant mobs of people storm the square, scale the monument, dance atop its pedestal, and shout the joyous cry of freedom: "*Vive le quatorze juillet!*" — Long live the 14th of July!

PARTY LIKE IT'S 1789

Place de la Bastille is only one of countless Bastille Day parties. All across Paris and in every town and village in France, July 13 is a night of joyful excess.

In fact, the best parties are on Paris' smaller neighborhood squares. These are the Firemen's Balls, sponsored by local fire stations to benefit charities. Everyone, even tourists, are welcome to join in, for the price of a small donation to charity. Food, drink, and music spill out into the street, and soon it's a block party. (Some fire stations get so jammed with revelers that, well, it's a good thing the fire marshal doesn't drop by.)

Elsewhere in Paris, there's plenty of live music. Bars, cafés, and outdoor stages feature big-name acts and small. One of Paris' biggest squares, Place de la Concorde, is known to host crowds of a hundred thousand or more.

Everywhere in the partying there are reminders of the Revolution. Some people wear the Phrygian cap of the original Bastille Stormers—a red, floppy, Smurf-like beanie that has symbolized liberty since the days of ancient Rome. Some get dressed up in crazy Revolutionary costumes, like a pompadoured Marie-Antoinette or a velvet-suited Louis. Others dress as Marianne—the fictional woman who represents liberty, reason, the nation of France, and the motto "Live free or die." From St. Geneviève to Joan of Arc to Marianne, France has always incarnated its national spirit in the female form.

Everywhere you'll see the blue, white, and red colors of the French flag (the *tricolore*). The flag comes from that fateful July 14, when the Bastille was stormed by Parisians sporting the red and blue colors of the city. When white was added (by the Revolutionary general Lafayette), it became the national flag. For Bastille Day, flags fly from balconies and people paint it on their faces. Military jets—the French version of the Blue Angels—fly overhead in formation, trailing blue-white-and-red smoke to paint the *tricolore* across the sky.

Revelers occasionally break out in song, singing the French National Anthem, the "Marseillaise." "*Allons enfants de la Patrie*," the stirring anthem begins. "Rise up, children of the fatherland, the day of glory has arrived!" It's a rousing tune,

OPPOSITE:

While Place de la Bastille hosts the city's biggest party, there are neighborhood fetes and patriotic displays all over Paris.

RIGHT:

"Allons enfants de la Patrie," *goes the national anthem.* "Rise up, children of the fatherland."

but, frankly, the lyrics are a bit edgy for today's genteel French. "To arms, citizens," it says, "let us march" to fight the tyrants—until "their impure blood waters our fields."

In fact, Bastille Day can have a kind of hard edge. It's when today's revolutionaries seize the day to make their voices heard. They march and demonstrate, turn over cars, throw rocks at police, and set fires—protesting today's tyrants. The fitful march toward universal liberty is an ongoing process.

The Revolution continues.

THE GRAND MILITARY PARADE DOWN THE CHAMPS-ELYSÉES

The next morning, on July 14, the festivities take on a more sober and patriotic aspect. That's when thousands line the Champs-Elysées for a grand military parade.

It's a spectacular setting. The Champs-Elysées is Europe's most renowned boulevard. It's one solid mile of broad sidewalks, stylish shops, elegant cafés, glimmering showrooms, and proud Parisians. Most days, it's home to shoppers, tourists, and people-watchers from across the globe. But on special occasions, the whole nation of France turns its focus here: to celebrate the end of wars, World Cup soccer triumphs, the finale of the Tour de France—and Bastille Day.

The parade starts sharply at 10:00 a.m. with a brief ceremony at the Tomb of the Unknown Soldier, at the base of the Arc de Triomphe. Europe's oldest parade stars France's various military units—Army, Navy, Air Force, and so on—wearing their various outfits, such as dress uniforms or camouflage-and-berets. There are veterans to be honored and tanks to show off, while helicopters hover overhead. Old-style cavalry soldiers ride on horseback with their feathered helmets and sabers.

The parade is attended by dignitaries and representatives from around the

world, from kilt-wearing Scots to half-naked Maoris. Traditionally, France's fellow Allies from World War I attend, including the US. The Yanks have always been grateful to France for its aid during the American Revolution, and the assistance of France's Marquis de Lafayette. America returned the favor in World Wars I and II, under the motto *"Lafayette, nous voilà"*—Lafayette, we are here.

The parade route itself is a constant reminder of the Revolution. It starts at the towering Arc de Triomphe, built to honor the Revolution's high-water mark, when France's citizen-army triumphed over Europe's monarchies. The Arc's most famous relief (*La Marseillaise*, by François Rude) depicts a ferocious Lady Liberty who points her fellow Revolutionaries to victory with her sword. The parade ends at Place de la Concorde, a grim reminder of the Revolution's darkest days. Here, a tall obelisk stands, marking the spot where once stood the most feared symbol of the Revolution—the guillotine.

PLACE DE LA CONCORDE
AND THE REIGN OF TERROR

The Storming of the Bastille touched off an extraordinary series of events.

Within weeks of July 14, France was in full Revolution mode. Uppity peasants were tenderizing their masters with pitchforks. The citizens' Assembly demolished feudalism, abolished Church privileges, and nationalized nobles' land. A mob of Parisian women marched on the lavish palace of Versailles and arrested King Louis XVI and Queen Marie-Antoinette.

The king—now known simply as Citizen Capet—was led to Place de la Concorde. There he was laid face down on a slab beneath the guillotine. Shoop! A thousand years of monarchy that dated back to before Charlemagne was decapitated. Shortly after, Marie-Antoinette also was led to Place de la Concorde. Genteel to the end, she apologized to the executioner for accidentally stepping on his foot. The blade fell, the blood gushed, and her head was shown to the crowd on a stick—an exclamation point for the new rallying cry: *"Vive la nation!"*

As the Revolution ground onward, more enemies of the Revolution were executed. Then it was the Revolutionaries themselves who were branded as "enemies of the people." The dreaded guillotine was given sardonic nicknames: "the national razor," "The Machine," and "Monsieur de Paris." For a year, the Revolution went through a spate of senseless executions called the Reign of Terror. Some 2,500 Parisians were instantly made "a head shorter at the top." The Terror only came to an end when the Revolutionary leader Robespierre—who'd sent so many others to their deaths—was himself arrested, tried, and beheaded. (The guillotine claimed its last victim in 1977, after which capital punishment was abolished in France.)

The worst of the Revolution was over. Into the chaos stepped a man who could restore order, a young Revolutionary general named Napoleon Bonaparte. He would pick up the torch of Revolution and carry it across Europe. The events of that fateful day on July 14, 1789, were now changing the course of history.

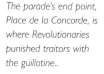

The parade's end point, Place de la Concorde, is where Revolutionaries punished traitors with the guillotine..

THE GLORIOUS CLIMAX—
FIREWORKS AT THE EIFFEL TOWER

The finale of Bastille Day unfolds at Paris' most iconic sight—the Eiffel Tower.

As evening descends on July 14, people start gathering on the lawn at the Champ de Mars park at the base of the Tower. They bring baguettes, cheese, fruit, and bottles of wine. It's low-key at first, but as darkness falls, the scene gets crowded and raucous.

Ironically, the very first anniversary of Bastille Day took place here where the Eiffel Tower stands today. It was July 14, 1790, and the Revolutionaries marked the one-year occasion with a festival they called *La Fête de la Fédération*. They gathered on the Champ de Mars and reflected on the incredible changes of the previous year. Imagine the jubilation! To shout out loud what had long been kept inside. Members of every social class gathered here to mingle equally, hugging

Crowds arrive early to picnic and get a spot to view the night's fireworks.

and kissing. Heroes of the Revolution ascended a makeshift altar to be honored. Women dressed up to symbolize Truth, Freedom, and Justice were worshipped in a new kind of secular religion. Fireworks lit up the night, and once-starving people feasted on rich food and fine wine. That first Bastille Day was a heady celebration of their new-found freedom: Liberty! Equality! Fraternity!

After that first anniversary, there was no official Bastille Day celebration for decades. But by the 1870s, after a disheartening war with Prussia, the French needed a boost to reestablish their self-identity. They remembered the proud days of 1789 that had birthed the republic, and marked it with banquets and military parades. Finally, in 1880, July 14 was proclaimed the French national holiday. It's officially named *La Fête Nationale* (The National Festival), but most French people simply call it by the date: *le quatorze juillet*.

In 1889, France celebrated the 100th anniversary of the Revolution by inviting the whole world to a world's fair—the *Exposition Universelle*. What would the

centerpiece of the fairground be? They considered various Revolutionary-themed proposals, including one for a giant guillotine. They finally decided on a more optimistic structure—the Eiffel Tower. It was a 1,000-foot proclamation of the French Revolution and of the bright future it had created for the whole world.

On July 14, as darkness descends on the Eiffel Tower, the excitement builds. By now, the Champ de Mars is packed. Nearby, people gather at every possible spot with a view of the Eiffel Tower: the Trocadero, on cruise-boats on the Seine, and packing the bridges and riverside quais. Lucky people with Tower views from their apartments invite friends over. All eyes turn toward the Tower. The lights come on and it glows golden. Next, they throw a switch, and it's suddenly glittering.

As midnight approaches, the Bastille Day festivities reach their climax. Oooh! Aaah! The phallic structure spurts fireworks, lighting up the night sky with dazzling colors. The event is witnessed by hundreds of thousands around the Tower. It's televised across France to millions more, and beamed across the globe, where the event is celebrated simultaneously in every time zone.

CELEBRATIONS ACROSS THE GLOBE

The Storming of the Bastille in 1789 transformed not only France, but many other nations, from medieval oppression to modern democracy. No wonder the holiday has become a global event. In countries around the world, French expats and emigrants gather to celebrate their roots. French embassies and consulates sponsor events as a gesture of international goodwill. Even non-French people see the allure, indulging in a day of world-class wines and cheeses, baguettes, pastries, *petanque*, music, and all things French. Anyone with a sense of history can recognize the enormous debt the world owes to those brave Parisians who stormed the Bastille. It's a cultural rallying point, symbolizing freedom of all kinds.

And so—while Parisians are rejoicing at the Eiffel Tower, Place de la Bastille, the Champs-Elysées, and in neighborhood parties around France—the rest of the world joins in. In Dublin, they set aside their Guinness for a day and sample French wines. In New Zealand, Auckland holds a big block party like those in Paris. New Orleans, which has deep French roots (can you say "French Quarter"?), hosts a number of events. In Milwaukee, they erect a four-story Eiffel Tower, while New York City lights up the Empire State Building in blue, white, and red. And in St. Louis (settled by French fur traders), they set up a guillotine, ceremonially decapitate Louis and Marie, and display their severed heads to the joyous crowd. How festive!

Vive la France!

Fireworks explode all over France—from the French Riviera to the Eiffel Tower—the perfect climax to a day celebrating the sheer joy of freedom.

HIGHLAND GAMES IN SCOTLAND

Highland Games—
A Day of Sports, Music, and Gaelic Pride

All across Scotland, communities big and small host a Highland Games. It's an all-day celebration of local sports and culture, like a track meet and a county fair rolled into one. The heart of the celebration is the various competitions where kilted Scots square off in athletics and dancing. But it's much more. It's a time for modern Scots to get together to celebrate all things Scottish, Gaelic, and Celtic—their culture, music, dancing, foods, arts, and traditions.

The Highland Games (also called a Highland Gathering) are generally held on weekend days from May to September. Some Games are big productions, lasting two or three days, with corporate sponsorship, grandstand seating, big-name entertainment, and advance tickets. The Cowal Highland Gathering draws 20,000 spectators and thousands of competitors, and Braemar's is attended by the British royals. But all across Scotland, in humble towns and villages, there are smaller Highland Games, where most anyone can walk right in and join in the fun. I've thoroughly enjoyed games in small towns—like Airth and Kenmore. For locals, it's a fine day out for the family, and a chance to remember their traditional roots and clan pride—all set to a soundtrack of Scottish music.

OPPOSITE:
The Games begin: Dancers assemble, clans congregate, athletes register for events, food stands appear, and bagpipers warm up.

The Day Begins

The Games open their gates around 9:00 in the morning. The setting can be humble—a grassy field at the town park, or a running track—or it can be spectacular, with a lush lawn, fir trees, craggy hillsides, a castle in the distance, or clouds hanging low over the mountains.

They've set up various stages for the music and dancing events. Meanwhile, vendors start assembling their food and souvenir tents. This is a day when local charities can raise funds by selling burgers, grilled sausages, and baked goods.

The first to arrive are the competitors, who come early to register. At the smaller games, it's pretty informal—just show up, pay a couple of pounds, get a number to pin to your kilt, and you're in. Spectators pay an admission fee of a few pounds, and start filing in. The games go on rain or shine, and locals come prepared and cheerful through any weather.

It's soon a festive scene. The grounds are dotted with colorful tents, flags in the wind, and locals in kilts and weekend wear. People browse the various booths, grazing on Scottish foods, county-fair-type junk food, and locally-brewed beer.

Many Games take place in a glorious setting in the lush and rugged Highlands.

Of course, there are always places to taste the Scottish national drink—whisky. There's also a popular soft drink called "Irn-Bru" ("Iron Brew") that bills itself as "Scotland's other national drink." (The orange-colored soda's hard-to-pin-down taste has been described as everything from citrus to cream soda to battery acid.)

As the name implies, the Games focus on the Highlands, the mountainous northwest region of Scotland. In this rugged land of steep hills and deep ravines punctuated by lakes (or "lochs"), a stubborn resistance to modern ways lives on. It's a mix of time-worn towns, venerable whisky distilleries, and desolate stone burial mounds as old as the pyramids. It's the land of legend and mystery—from Loch Ness monsters to Brigadoon villages to a wizarding school called Hogwarts. Many Scottish icons originated here in the Highlands, from kilts to bagpipes to the Games that bring them all together.

Around noon, the sporting events begin, kicked off with—what else?—bagpipes. A band of pipers and drummers marches in and parades around the field,

The Games commence
with a marching bagpipe
band.

often led by the local clan chieftain. A local emcee welcomes everyone, setting a festive tone in a lilting Scottish accent. Spectators start finding a good viewing spot—in bleachers, on a hillside, or just standing along the sidelines.

Let the Games begin.

THE HEAVY EVENTS

The core of every Highland Games is always the so-called "heavy events." This is where brawny athletes test their ability to hurl various objects of awkward shapes and sizes as far as possible. Some of these events are very old, and may be the inspiration for similar events still done today in modern Olympic times. But unlike the Olympics, there's a rule aimed specifically at the big boys in the heavy events: "Kilts must be worn during the competition."

The "stone put" is an archaic version of the shot put, where they throw a round stone or metal ball. Like Olympic shot-putters, there's usually a 16-pound event, but there's also a more robust 22-pound one. There's the hammer throw. Kilted Highlanders spin like bulky ballerinas and release a 28- or 56-pound ball attached to a chain or solid shaft. In the "weight over the bar" event, competitors try to throw a 56-pound weight over a horizontal bar that can be up to 15 feet high—like tossing a five-year-old over a double-decker bus.

A local favorite involves lifting a beloved boulder dubbed the "manhood stone." Big lads down a wee glass of courage and try to impress their lassies. They have to lift the huge (roughly 250-pound) stone off the ground, then waddle forward to see who can carry it the farthest.

And, of course, there's the caber toss. They first have to pick the giant log up— it's 20 feet long and weighs 175 pounds. Then they have to flip it over, end-over-end. The idea is to do it in one coordinated motion: Pick the log up, point it straight up, get a running start, then throw. You have to flip it all the way over,

Burly men in kilts do the hammer throw and the caber toss, in which they try to flip the log forward to land in a straight line.

directly in front of you, to land flat on the ground. For this game, it's not who throws it the farthest but whose log lands the straightest. Judges measure if it's at "12 o'clock" (perfectly in line) or to the left or right (like 10:00 or 2:00 o'clock). Frankly, it's a wonder anyone can even lift the heavy log, much less flip it, much less avoid a hernia.

Meanwhile, like a three-ring circus, other events are going on simultaneously elsewhere.

Runners in shorts and tank tops race around the track. These events are like track meets everywhere—the 90-meter dash, the 1,600-meter, and so on. The Games might give it a local spin, like a 5K that races up a nearby hillside. Another popular event is "hill running" (also called fell running), which involves racing cross-country through the hills, usually off-road and without trails. Different distances and gradients help determine the difficulty of the runs.

Some events are for men, for women, for kids, and some events are open to all. Entry fees are nominal—just a couple of pounds. The Games are pretty informal and all in good fun, though organizers warn: "Random drug tests may be taken." The winners take home a shiny trophy, plus enough cash to buy the lads a round at the local pub.

The Games Through the Centuries

The origins of the Highland Games are lost in the mists of time.

Most likely, they started among soldiers exercising and training for battle. We know this is true for, say, the warriors of ancient Greece who created the first Olympic Games. Legends say the first Scottish footraces date back a thousand years, when the king staged a competition to choose his personal mailman. The first shot put might have started with warriors throwing heavy stones at their enemies. Regardless, as the centuries wore on, the Games became a spectator sport. Villages staged them at market time or for the annual county fair. Itinerant laborers competed for jobs by tossing bales of hay, while Romeos won sweethearts with their bulging muscles. Ultimately, the Games evolved into that time-honored human pastime known as just having fun. It was an occasion to play music (and bagpipes). People danced and feasted on good food and drink.

The Highland Games really came of age in the late 1800s. They were part of a joyous revival of Highland culture after an especially bitter time of hardship.

You see, Scotland had come under the thumb of the British nation. Then in the year 1745, Scotland rose in revolt, led by Highlanders under the dashing Bonnie Prince Charlie. His ragtag, kilted, bagpipe-bolstered army of 6,000 swept southward, driving the British troops nearly back to London. The British fought back. They finally cornered the Scots at the Battle of Culloden, where the Highlanders were routed and massacred.

Scotland was brutally punished—particularly the Highlands. Kilts were banned. The Gaelic language was suppressed and clan chieftains stripped of power. Scots were driven from their lands and their homes burned—a sad event called "the Highland Clearances." Farmers and villages were replaced by sheepherders and factories. Highlanders moved south to cities in the Lowlands

The Highlands is the most independently "Scottish" region. Bonnie Prince Charlie tried to resist English domination, but the Highlanders were defeated and exiled.

(Glasgow, Edinburgh) to find menial work. Some two million Scots fled the country completely—to the US, Canada, Australia, and New Zealand. It looked like traditional Highland culture had been snuffed out.

But Highland culture was revived. In the 1800s—the era of Romanticism—everything Scottish was now celebrated in a nostalgic embrace. Queen Victoria bought a Scottish castle (Balmoral), and Bonnie Prince Charlie became the hero of a popular novel. Kilts, tartans, and bagpipes were suddenly trendy.

This was when the Highland Games were organized as we know them now. It was a way to promote and preserve Scottish culture. And since then, they've only grown. These days, it's a way for ordinary Scots to commemorate their history, patriotic pride, and independence from Britain, while passing these values on to the next generation.

In fact, "Highland Games" are now a worldwide phenomenon—from the States, to Canada, to Australia. It seems everyone wants a little taste of Scotland. And millions of little girls everywhere sign up for classes to practice their twinkle-toes Highland Dances.

The Highland Dancers

While sweaty brutes in kilts throw weights at one end of the field, at the other end are little girls in skirts locked in their own competition. These are the Highland Dancers.

The girls gather around the stage and warm up. They're dressed in their peasant blouses, tartan skirts, long plaid stockings, and lace-up slippers. Then, as their name is called, they each take their turn on the stage. The dancers compete solo, or in groups of two or four, and are generally accompanied by a lone bagpiper.

Highland dancing is highly technical, involving precise footwork. They leap and prance and kick, with their toes pointed. They must dance only on the balls of their feet, requiring excellent balance and stamina. Dancers raise one arm and put the other hand on their hip as they step, spin, and twirl. They toe their routines with intense concentration. Most competitors are female—from wee lassies barely out of nappies, all the way to confident professionals. They're judged on their poise, the height of their jumps, how well they stay in time to the music, their arm-and-hand gestures, and even "Best Dressed."

There are many different dance events. In the popular dance called the Highland Fling, the goal is to keep the feet as close as possible to one spot. In the Sword Dances, they have to step gingerly over two crossed swords placed on the stage.

The origins of Highland Dancing are obscure, but we know they were originally danced by men. The Highland Fling, for example, may have been a courtship dance, where men imitated the movements of a rutting stag. The Sword Dances were started by soldiers. It may have been a kind of victory celebration—like doing a touchdown dance over your enemy's weapons. Or they might have been danced on the eve of battle to ensure good luck. Or as a training exercise, stepping between the swords to learn the intricate footwork of sword-fighting.

Wee lassies compete in Highland Dancing events—always a highlight.

Highland Dancing became a part of the Highland Games when they were revived in the late 1800s. Since then, the dances have become more eclectic. Women joined in, and now it's 90 percent female. There are now folk dances from other countries, like the Jig (from Ireland) and the Hornpipe (from English sailors). The exuberant dancers have become emblematic of the sheer joy of the Highland Games.

PIPERS—A BATTLE OF THE BANDS

No Scottish event would be complete without bagpipes.

The bagpipes—a droning instrument made from a sack of animal skins—are ancient. The Scottish bagpipes were born in the Highlands during late-medieval times. They were used on the battlefield to rouse the hearts of the hardy Scots and send their music-loving enemies running for their lives.

For the Highland Games, pipers and drummers come from all over Scotland to compete. There are group events for marching bands, plus competitions for solo

Solo pipers and marching bands square off to see who's best.

pipers and drummers. The events cover many kinds of traditional bagpipe songs, dance tunes (reels and jigs), military salutes, battle songs, and graceful romantic airs.

The Games always open with the entry of the pipers and drummers. They play at "halftime" between the various other games. They provide the perfect audio landscape for the day's events.

HERDING SHEEP, GATHERING CLANS, AND HURLING HAGGIS

Most Highland Games have plenty of other activities besides sports, dancing, and piping.

For the kids there are gunnysack races and test-your-skill carnival games. There might be men with old-time swords, recreating famous battles in Scottish history. Breeders show off their dogs' sheepherding skills. You can pet Highland cattle, with their thick furry coats and long horns. Musicians play harps. There are old-

Other events at the Games might include sheepdog shows or battle reenactments (maybe this time, the Scots might win).

time sports like shinty (Scottish field hockey), and modern elements, like a classic car show.

One popular new "sport" is haggis hurling. Haggis is a local delicacy made of a sheep's stomach stuffed with the sheep's own diced organs. Participants stand on a whisky barrel and throw the round haggis as far as possible. (What else, many wonder, is it good for?)

Like festivals everywhere, the grounds are filled with tents and booths of local vendors. You can taste whisky, or buy tartan ties, Loch Ness potholders, and kilted bottle openers.

The Games have become a modern "gathering of the clans." Before there was a united nation of Scotland, it was ruled by extended families called clans—the MacGregors and MacKenzies, the Macleods, Campbells, and Frasers. Today, the descendants of these clans use the Games to keep their family heritage alive. They set up tents proudly decorated with their coats of arms. They wear kilts with their distinct family colors and patterns (called tartans). They welcome their fellow Drummonds and Kincaids and MacDonalds. They invite people in who find themselves clan-less in the modern world, and encourage them to

It's a time to show off your Scottish pride, from tartans to family ties.

check their genealogy, reconnect with their roots, and join the big extended family that is Scotland.

THE GAMES COME TO AN END

As the late-afternoon shadows get longer, the Games build to their big finale. It might be an event where everyone can join in, like a town-wide tug-of-war that leaves everybody muddy, sore, and laughing hysterically.

Then the Games officially end with—you guessed it—more bagpipes. All of the pipe and drum bands gather together for a "massing of the bands." They join up to play a tune everyone knows—something like "Amazing Grace," "Highland Laddie," or "Scotland the Brave." With pipes playing, drummers drumming, and

The Games end with another bagpipe parade that might lead everyone into town.

a drum-major marching proudly in front, they circle the field one last time. Then they head off into town with people in tow to parade through the streets.

Then everyone disperses into the pubs. Here they begin the traditional *ceilidh* (KAY-lee)—a get-together of music, talk, and good times. The winners celebrate with beers and whisky, and the losers celebrate with beers and whisky. The guitars, fiddles, accordions, and tin whistles come out, all driven to the beat of the hand-drum called the *bodhrán*. All across town, the happy sound of traditional folk music spills out into the streets. Eyes get misty, as tunes both happy and sad are sung. You can see the tumult of the past and the love of heritage in the singers' eyes. There really is a spark that comes out only with that unique mix of beer, smiles, celebrating cultural traditions, and the ambience of a pub. Sipping a local brew, surrounded by Scottish conviviality—it's the perfect end to the Highland Games.

Cap off the day at the corner pub, with a whisky, local ale, and a Gaelic singalong.

OKTOBERFEST IN MUNICH

Oktoberfest—Deutschland at Play

Every year, Munich hosts the planet's biggest kegger—Oktoberfest. It's happened ever since 1810, when the Bavarian king threw a big public wedding reception. It was such a hit that they decided to do it again the next year. And the next, and the next. Two hundred years later, it's become one of Europe's biggest and best-known festivals—a beer-fueled frenzy of dancing, music, food, and amusements.

Oktoberfest lasts for 16 days, from the third Saturday in September to the first Sunday in October. It takes place on a vast fairground outside Munich's city center. It's easy for any visitor to enjoy. Admission is free. (Of course, food, drink, and carnival rides are extra.) It's a slap-happy world of lederhosen, dirndls, fancy hats, and maidens with flowers in their hair. For a visitor, there's no better place to see (and join) Germans at play.

Munich is a major metropolis with a medieval ambience, shown here in its main square—Marienplatz.

Munich—
A Global Village Built for Locals

In the days leading up to Oktoberfest, visitors from around the globe start pouring into Munich. (Last-minute hotel rooms can be hard to find, so book ahead.)

While there are plenty of tourists, Oktoberfest is still very much a local scene. It's estimated that 90 percent of the attendees are Bavarians. It's where they come to have fun in a way they've done for two centuries.

Men put on their lederhosen. These are the leather shorts with suspenders once worn by peasants working the fields. They accessorize with long stockings and a hat with a feather in it. Women wear their dirndl—a single-piece dress that includes a skirt and low-cut blouse, covered with a bodice. These traditional Bavarian clothes are not mere party costumes worn ironically. Locals treasure them, and break them out on special occasions.

Locals break out their traditional dirndls and lederhosen—not out of place in the "village" of Munich.

Oktoberfest is a festival of Bavarian culture. The state of Bavaria (of which Munich is the capital) is home to many of the cultural clichés we've come to associate with Germany. That means beer, lederhosen, alpine scenery, and a laid-back, happy-go-lucky lifestyle. These have become German clichés, but they are Bavarian. And in Bavaria they still live on.

Even in Bavaria's big city of Munich, they try hard to maintain old ways amid the bustle of modern life. The city itself looks medieval, though it's not. Munich's Old Town was bombed to smithereens in World War II. Whereas other cities like Frankfurt rebuilt with skyscrapers, Munich made a conscious decision to preserve its medieval heritage. Today it's a modern hub of international commerce and corporate headquarters, but much of it is housed behind quaint Bavarian facades. Munich is still a city of pedestrian streets, leafy beer gardens, and a large park where locals go to jog, picnic, surf (true, but too hard to explain right now), and frolic in the nude (yes, also true).

Year after year, Munich always ranks high on the lists of the world's most-livable cities. Locals still think of their city as a small community, like a tight-knit Bavarian town. They proudly nickname their metropolis *"Millionendorf"*—the village of a million people.

Oktoberfest is a celebration of the laid-back Bavarian lifestyle that includes beer gardens and surfing at the English Garden.

PARTY PREPARATIONS—
GERMAN ENGINEERING AT WORK

Putting on Oktoberfest is a vast undertaking, but the super-organized Germans pull it off with ease. Each year, in the weeks leading up to Oktoberfest, trucks and construction workers pour into the fairground for the set-up.

Oktoberfest is staged in a Disneyland-sized field south of the main train station, called Theresienwiese. This was where that first Oktoberfest happened back in 1810, with the wedding of Ludwig I—grandfather of "Mad" King Ludwig II of castle-building fame. His bride was Duchess Therese, and the meadow was named in her honor— "Theresa's Meadow." Over the years, locals have shortened the meadow's name to "Wies'n" (VEE-zen). In fact, locals tend to call the Oktoberfest festival itself "the Wies'n."

It's here that they set up the huge Oktoberfest "tents"—or so they're called, though they aren't soft-canvas circus tents. They're semi-permanent structures of wood, steel, and glass, similar to county-fair pavilions. Once assembled, each of these will hold several thousand beer drinkers. Forklifts haul in the beams, and cherry-picker cranes hoist carpenters up to screw them together. They set up the

The event takes place at a fairground (once a meadow), first inaugurated by the dashing King Ludwig I.

various shacks for vendors, and schlep in thousands of boxes of food, beer, and souvenirs. Decorations go up—man-sized plastic pretzels, huge garlands, and illuminated beer mugs. The beerhall tents are surrounded by dozens of amusement park rides that need to be readied for operation. Watching over the whole Theresienwiese is a monument that's been here since the days of King Ludwig—a 60-foot bronze statue of Lady Bavaria with the lion of Munich.

All this prep goes on with typical German efficiency. Despite all the craziness and crowds, Munich's downtown is actually pretty sane, and it's a good time to sightsee. Everywhere, security is very tight, but it feels relaxed. No wonder it's all so well organized—they've been at it every year for 200 years.

Opening Ceremonies— A Parade and Tapping the First Keg

The festivities kick off around 10:00 in the morning with a grand parade, starting in downtown Munich and heading for the Wies'n.

With more than 5,000 participants, the parade seems endless. There are marching bands and paraders dressed in colorful traditional costumes, representing every corner of Bavarian society. Munich's famed "coopers" (barrel makers) do their traditional dance made famous by the spinning statues of Munich's glockenspiel. There are representatives from across the globe—marching bands, folk dancers, and brightly dressed troupes.

The main attraction is the traditional beer wagons. Massive, elaborately decorated draft horses clop by, pulling wagons filled with huge kegs of draft beer. Each of the city's main breweries enters a beer-themed float to entertain the crowds as they make their way to the festival grounds.

At the head of the parade is the festival queen—the Münchner Kindl. This "Munich Child" is the symbol of the city. This is a young woman on horseback, wearing the robe of a medieval monk.

You see, the city got its name from the original inhabitants who settled here—the monks, or *Mönchen*. And its budding economy was fueled by a popular product manufactured by monks—beer. In medieval Munich, there were more than 30 breweries pumping out the liquid gold. They stored their beer in cellars under their monastery courtyards kept cool by the shade of bushy chestnut trees. That beer tradition continues in Munich to this day. For Oktoberfest, the city's monk becomes a teenage girl hoisting beer. She serves as a kind of Miss Oktoberfest, presiding over various ceremonies, starting with the opening parade.

The parade arrives at Thereseienwiese. Eager, thirsty revelers fill the enormous tents awaiting the grand opening. The mayor ascends a dais. At exactly noon, he ceremonially opens the first keg. "*O'zapft is!*" he announces to the crowd—"It's tapped." Mugs of beer are filled and passed to other dignitaries to take the first sips. Now, all across the fairground, the tents can start serving beer.

Another Oktoberfest begins.

Festivities begin with a long parade (starring the Münchner Kindl) through Munich and out to the fairground.

A Tent of One's Own—
From Oompah to Opera

For the next 16 days, it's a beer-fueled frenzy of hearty food, live music, and carnival rides. Beer is served from morning till night. Total strangers stroll arm-in-arm down rows of picnic tables, while beer maids pull mustard packs from their cleavage.

Revelers can choose from around 15 different tents. These operate like pop-up beerhalls. They're vast spaces, filled with row after row of wooden tables and benches, that can each hold up to 7,000 people.

The first keg is tapped, and revelers crowd into the enormous "tents"— pop-up beer halls.

Although beer-drinking is the main event, Oktoberfest is for families, too, with carnival rides and easygoing socializing.

gebrannte
Mandeln
00 g 2,50
50 g 5,-

Each tent has its own personality. Some are decorated in a traditional way, with the Bavarian colors of white and blue. They may have colorful maypoles out front, like in a Bavarian small-town square. The walls may have faux half-timbering, or leafy garlands hanging from the ceiling, suggesting an open-air beer garden. These traditional tents offer traditional oompah music—an ensemble of brass, woodwinds, accordion, and drums.

Other tents cater to the rowdy youth, with a rock band playing. Yet another tent might advertise its menu—their roast suckling pig, mackerel on a stick, or their potato salad just like *Mutter* used to make. Some tents offer a change of pace with a range of fine wines. Others bill themselves as especially *gemütlich*—cozy and convivial. Still others are more family-friendly, with kids' menus and prices.

Each of Munich's leading breweries sponsors a tent. These tents take on the character of their sister beerhall in town. So, the Hofbräuhaus tent will be raucous and packed with tourists from around the world, while Spaten's is the opera-goers' tent, with a quieter setting and ox on the spit.

With so many choices, it's party time for about 14 hours a day, for 16 straight days. The fun rages day and night. Rivers of beer are drunk and tons of food are eaten. If you add up all the tents, there might be 100,000 partiers drinking a toast simultaneously at any given moment.

THE OKTOBERFEST SCENE

Even though the beer tents are gigantic, they're often full, especially on weekends. The atmosphere is thick. Live music plays, whether rock or traditional oompah bands. The walls might sport fun "eat, drink, and be merry" themes. "*Durst ist schlimmer als Heimweh*," is one common saying—"Thirst is worse than homesickness."

First-timers might find all the chaos a bit daunting. But Oktoberfest is, by its very nature, open and friendly. It's actually easy for foreigners to join in. The scene is least crowded and tamest Monday through Thursday in the late afternoon and early evening. Here you'll find families with kids enjoying a meal and the amusement rides. (Late at night it can get rougher and less family-friendly.) At night and on weekends, the most popular tents can fill up and have long waiting lines. But if a table is full, just wait for an opening and take a seat—it's tradition that anyone can sit at any table that can fit an extra rear end. Start a conversation with a toast and clink of your beer glass. At Oktoberfest, it's best to just take a deep breath, and dive headlong into the sudsy mosh pit.

Music is everywhere. People sing along and sway their beer mugs in time to the music. You'll certainly hear the classic drinking song called "Ein Prosit," or

Munich makes some of the world's best beer, and locals drink it from one-liter mugs.

Oompah bands fuel singalongs, while power-lifting waitresses fuel the singers.

"a toast." The song's lyrics propose a toast to *Gemütlichkeit*, prompting everyone to take another drink. Another classic beerhall tune has a shout-along refrain of "*Eins, Zwei, G'suffa*"—meaning "One, two . . . Drink up!"

A few American pop songs have become classic German drinking songs. The one everybody in Germany seems to know is the song "Country Roads." You'll hear Germans belting it out in English, along with "Sweet Caroline," and lots of German pop songs like the 80s classic "99 Luftballons."

Fast-moving waitresses with power-lifting bodices hoist armloads of heavy beer glasses. With their low-cut dirndls, it's a kind of Bavarian "Hooters." The waitresses are generally amateur servers working other jobs who spend their two-week vacation at Oktoberfest to make some serious extra money. They work as independent contractors. They "buy" the beer and pretzels at a wholesale price from the tent owners, and pocket the mark-up.

These pop-up beerhall tents come ready for anything. Security personnel make sure drunks don't get out of hand. Plenty of urinals accommodate the masses. And, in the saucy spirit of this festival, the men's bathrooms sport posters of randy girls in dirndls, commenting on what they see.

After a few beers, people head outside and stroll the happy central promenade,

through a carnival of rides—roller-coasters, merry-go-rounds, kiddie rides, and daredevil attractions. There's a huge Ferris wheel. The five-loops roller coaster must be the wildest on earth. (Locals advise it's best done before the beer.)

Everywhere, locals and tourists mingle. With tens of thousands of people roaming the grounds, it's a multigenerational, multicultural playground where fun is the universal language.

The tents provide for every need, from security staff for handling drunks, to peek-a-boo urinals.

THE BEST BEER AND THE WURST FOOD

The average German drinks 27 gallons of beer a year. And Bavaria, the heart of beer country, is where large beerhalls and beer gardens originated. In fact, the world's oldest food law—the Reinheitsgebot, or German Beer Purity Law of 1516—actually came from Bavaria. It stipulated that beer could only consist of three ingredients—barley, hops, and water—with no additives. Why was beer treated with such respect? Because back then, it was considered liquid food, and also, safe drinking water was hard to come by.

Munich has six major breweries with a long history. The list includes a few names that have gone on to become world-famous. There's the Hofbräu which, as the name suggests, was the personal brewery (*bräu*) of the Bavarian royal court (*hof*). When the Hofbräu's 5,000-seat beer hall was flattened in World War II, it was one of the first structures rebuilt and became a favorite of US servicemen. Other famous breweries in Munich include Löwenbräu, Augustiner, and Spaten, which now produce export beer sold worldwide.

At Oktoberfest, people come not only to drink but to eat. They might snack on a *Brez'n* (a pretzel) or a *Radi*—a radish that's thinly spiral-cut and salted. *Brotzeit* ("bread time") is a Bavarian phrase for a between-meal snack of cold cuts, cheese, and bread. Snackers can also choose from hundreds of varieties of sausages (*Wurst*), served with a roll or with sauerkraut (even if you've never liked sauerkraut, you've got to try it here). What's the best of the *Wurst*? Well, if it's late-morning, Oktoberfest revelers prefer the local *Weisswurst*—white sausage—served with mustard, a pretzel, and a beer.

Locals also come to Oktoberfest for high-quality lunches and dinners. Bavarians love pork knuckle (*Schweinshax'n*), meatballs (*Fleischpflanzerl*), and mackerel on a stick (*Steckerlfisch*). These are served with a side of sauerkraut, dumplings, noodles, potatoes, or an excellent salad. And for dessert—how about a slice of *Apfelstrudel?*

There's surprisingly good food, especially Bavarian specialties: snacks of Weisswurst *and pretzels,* Schweinshax'n *and sauerkraut, and—for dessert—* Apfelstrudel.

But for most Oktoberfest revelers, it's all about the beer. Beer maids keep it coming. Traditionally, Germans have drunk their beer from old steins made of pottery and pewter. But during Oktoberfest, they use the more efficient glass mugs. The standard serving is a huge mug called *eine Mass*—one liter. That's about a quart (or what Americans might call "ein pitcher.") I once asked if they sell half-liters. "This is a *Biergarten*," I was told. "Not a kindergarten."

Famous beer halls in town—like Löwenbräu and the Hofbräuhaus— each sponsor a tent at the fairground.

It Ain't Over Till the Last Ox is Roasted

Oktoberfest reaches its peak on the final weekend. The last Saturday is often the busiest day. Last chance to ride the roller coaster. Last chance to try Munich's best potato salad. Last chance to belt out "Country Roads" before they take you home. On that last night, the Wies'n is an illuminated wonderland of glittering amusement park rides and lit-up revelers.

It's been a crazy event. When it's all over, the organizers tally up the numbers: Six million visitors consumed 7 million liters of beer, a half-million chickens, and 100 oxen.

And they'll do it all again next year.

CHRISTMAS

'TIS THE SEASON

AS AUTUMN DARKENS into winter, it's time for Europe's most brilliant festival season: Christmas.

Europe is my favorite place to travel, and Christmas is my favorite holiday. Christmas in Europe is observed by Christians as the time to remember the birth of Jesus on December 25.

It's a season of joy—full of bright lights, sweet foods, gift-giving, and lots of fun for the kids. With the calendar year reaching its close, Christmas becomes a time to reflect on the past year and anticipate the next.

In Europe, Christmas is more than just a day—it's a season, starting a month before Christmas Day and extending nearly two weeks beyond.

The season kicks off in early December with Advent, the day that anticipates the coming "arrival" (advent) of the baby Jesus. In Europe, this truly is the start of the Christmas season, since advertisers are reluctant to commercialize it any ear-

Christmas is celebrated all over Europe with bright lights, like along the Champs-Elysées.

lier. Next up is the Feast of St. Nicholas, celebrated with lots of gift giving around December 6. December 13 brings Santa Lucia Day, a festival promising the return of the light. Then comes Christmas itself. For many Europeans, Christmas Eve is the main event, celebrated with a midnight church service and a grand meal. Others concentrate on Christmas Day with its family time and gift giving. After December 25, lesser festivities continue through the "Twelve Days of Christmas"—from Boxing Day to New Year's to the gift-giving of Epiphany.

All of Europe gets into the spirit in one way or another. But each country, culture, and family puts a different emphasis on the various holidays and a different spin on the various traditions. In this chapter, I'll cover several of Europe's endearing Christmas traditions, but first, let's delve into the past.

THE ORIGINS OF CHRISTMAS

Christians remember the season for the birth of Jesus, and his adoration by shepherds and kings.

The Christmas festival is ancient. It's been celebrated for at least 2,000 years as the birthday of Jesus. Jesus was born in a humble barn, adored by nearby shepherds, praised by angels, and visited by Wise Men from the East bearing gifts. He would grow up to be the long-awaited Messiah, or Christ—the Light of the World who would redeem mankind from darkness and death.

But the festival goes back even further. The ancient Romans had long celebrated the season as "Saturnalia"—a wild and crazy midwinter toga party. They feasted and drank, gave gifts, partied by torchlight, and decorated homes with evergreen wreaths. When Christianity overtook pagan Rome, it made sense for the Christian fathers to dovetail the two celebrations together.

Even further back in time, this was the oldest human festival of all—the winter solstice. This day (usually December 21) is the darkest, coldest time of year. But it comes with the promise that the sun will soon return. Prehistoric pagans celebrated the solstice with traditions that we still observe today. They venerated evergreen trees, and decorated their temples with evergreen boughs, holly, ivy, and mistletoe as symbols of everlasting life during the barrenness of winter. They lit bonfires and kept a Yule log burning continuously to brighten this dark season. Over time the solstice became the joyful Saturnalia which became Christian Christmas—celebrating the arrival of the Son (of God), who brought spiritual light in the darkness.

Even Santa Claus has ancient ancestors in his family tree. He's descended from the prehistoric pagan god Odin—a bearded man who, at the solstice, rode through the sky on his magical horse, to find out who was naughty and nice. The British Celts had the lovable Frost King, a jolly holly-clothed man. Christians venerated

Some traditions date back to pre-Christian times, like evergreen trees (symbolic of life in barren winter) and the descendant of pagan Odin, Santa Claus.

a kindly gift-giving 3rd-century bishop named St. Nicholas. Over the centuries, these myths merged and morphed together into a variety of "Santa"-like figures. The English have their Father Christmas, and he's Pere Noel in France. He's Samichlaus in Switzerland and Sinterklaas in the Netherlands. They commonly wear red robes, furs, and hoods; have white hair and beards; and are known for being fun-loving—either bringing gifts to good kids or playfully punishing the naughty.

As the world has expanded and globalized, Christmas traditions have cross-pollinated. In the 19th century, classic "Christmas tree" customs born in Norway and Germany became popular in Victorian England. German customs spread to America with the wave of immigrants. In the 20th century, America's more commercialized Christmas customs bounced back to Europe. Christmas traditions that first began thousands of years ago continue to evolve. In 500 years, what will Santa be like?

Norway's Festival of Light in Darkness

Norwegians have a special place in their hearts for December 13, the feast day of Santa Lucia, a third-century martyr. She was a young Sicilian Christian of noble lineage, living when the pagan Romans were persecuting Christians. The legend says that St. Lucy would secretly go out at night, traveling from farm to farm, bringing baked goods to feed persecuted Christians hiding in the nearby catacombs. She was always dressed in a white gown with a red sash. To light her way, she wore a crown of lingonberry twigs holding blazing candles. She was arrested by the Romans and met her fate on December 13—traditionally considered the longest night of the year. (The actual solstice is around December 21, but the 13th is the day when the sun sets earliest at Norwegian latitudes.) Lucy's legend lived on, as did her all-too-appropriate name, which means "light."

Today, Santa Lucia Day is celebrated at family gatherings, churches, schools, day-care centers, nursing homes, and hospitals. In comes a procession of girls, led by a young girl as St. Lucy—the *Lussibrud*, or Lucy bride. She's dressed in a white robe, a crown of lights on her head, and a candle in her hand. The other girls carry baskets of saffron buns or ginger cookies to hand out. They may sing "Santa Lucia"—the same song popular in Italy but with Norwegian lyrics. As they sing, the girls parade in with their candles, as if to spread light to the world.

On Santa Lucia Day, angelic Norwegians wear crowns of light-bringing candles in honor of an ancient saint.

One of my most heartwarming moments in Norway was a Santa Lucia Day in a small-town senior center, which has housed widows and seniors for more than 200 years. Kindergarteners paraded in, led by a tiny blonde Lucia wearing her crown of lights. They passed out the saffron buns, served with steaming coffee. You could see in the seniors' glowing eyes that the sights, sounds, and smells brought back childhood memories. It also kicked off lifelong memories for these kids. Endearing rituals like these ensure that traditions stay strong from generation to generation. Lucia symbolizes hope and light amid the darkness, and during winter's darkest days, this celebration lightens the hearts of all who experience it.

NÜRNBERG—
THE ULTIMATE GERMAN CHRISTMAS MARKET

Cradling a cup of hot-spiced wine as a hand warmer, I strolled through the main square of a quintessential German town. All around me were bundled-up shoppers and kids sampling fresh gingerbread, riding the carousel, listening to roving

German towns like Nürnberg set up colorful Christmas markets in the main square.

brass quintets, and marveling at the newest toys. Spicy smoke billowed from bratwurst stalls.

It's a Christkindlesmarkt—Christmas market—where shoppers come to browse for that perfect gift or Christmas ornament. Many German cities open up their main square during December to host these outdoor markets. The most famous—with some 200 wooden stalls and 2 million visitors—is in the heartland of German Christmas, the Bavarian city of Nürnberg (Nuremberg).

Here you can see the various toys, foods, and decorations that really "say" Christmas. Germany practically invented many of our signature Christmas traditions. The practice of decorating Christmas trees with ornaments, candies, or candles developed in Germany in the 1500s. Germany also gave us enduring carols like "O Tannenbaum."

And there are the toys. Germany's most popular toy is the nutcracker. These small wooden figurines are practical (to crack nuts) or just decorative. Since they must be strong enough to crack nuts, these are usually authority figures like soldiers, police officers, and constables. Other figurines are "Smokers"—woodworkers, loggers, postmen, or peasants who send out fragrant incense from their tiny smoke-ring-blowing mouths.

As a traditional center for toy-making in Germany, Nürnberg has long prided

The shelves are stocked with traditional German Christmas trinkets, from handmade ornaments to the classic Christmas toy—nutcrackers.

itself on the quality of its Christmas market. With no canned music, fake greenery, plastic kitsch, or war toys, it feels classier than your average crafts fair. The merchants' stalls are old-style wood huts with traditional ambience, and each year the most beautiful stall is awarded the prestigious "Prune Man" trophy, a homemade figurine made of dried fruit. Hovering above it all is the market's symbol—the golden Rausch Angel. The name is an example of German onomatopoeia—"*rausch*" is the sound of wind blowing through the angel's gold foil wings. For locals, there's no better way to cap their Christmas tree than with a miniature version of this angel.

The Christkindlesmarkt also features iconic Christmas foods, many of them largely invented in Germany. (But blame the Italians for fruitcake.) Bakeries crank out traditional gingerbread, whether as a spiced cake, cookie, or small loaf. The traditional *Lebkuchen Nürnberg* is made with the same recipe used in the 17th century, when Nürnberg was the gingerbread capital of the world. Back then, gingerbread was not baked at home, but was made exclusively by a guild of master bakers. They employed the best woodcarvers to whittle intricate wooden molds of hearts, angels, and wreaths. Well-known painters frosted the cookies with flourishes to create works of art. Germany's gingerbread tradition subsequently spread throughout Europe and the world.

Shoppers feast on hot-spiced wine and Nürnberg's world-famous gingerbread.

At another stall, you can wrap your mittens around a mug of hot-spiced wine. The process of simmering ("mulling") wine with spices goes back to ancient Roman times. Here in Nürnberg, drinking the traditional beverage from a Styrofoam cup would ruin the experience, so you pay a deposit for a nicely decorated ceramic one. Either return the mug or keep it as a collectible, since each year there's a different model.

Another Christmas tradition that originated in Germany is the candy cane. The first candy canes were simple, straight, white sticks of sugar candy. In 1670, a German choirmaster invented the shepherd-crook shape and passed them out to restless kids to keep them quiet at church. Germans took to decorating their Christmas trees with them, and German immigrants brought the custom to America. It was an American candy company of the 1920s that added the signature red stripes now seen everywhere.

Strolling the Christkindlesmarkt, it's clear that Germany has long celebrated Christmas well. Their markets seem more like a public service than a commercial enterprise. They're a festive swirl of heartwarming sights, sparkling lights, Christmas carols, and fragrant scents. Nürnberg's Christkindlesmarkt (and its hot-spiced wine) really warms up the cold days, lights up the dark nights, and gets everyone into the holiday spirit.

ITALIANS—A WAY WITH A MANGER

Christmas season in Rome has a relaxed feel. The air is crisp, and stylish big-city Italians are bundled up with panache as they browse the shops.

Italians celebrate one particular Christmas tradition with special gusto—Nativity scenes, or *presepi*. These small scenes depict the stable where Jesus was born. The star is the little statue of the baby Jesus laid in a manger. He's attended by other figurines—his mother Mary, Joseph, cows, donkeys, adoring shepherds, and Wise Men.

One of Rome's classic squares, Piazza Navona, gets a visit from Signore Claus. Italians love creative creches of the Nativity.

These Christmas creches were first popularized 800 years ago by St. Francis of Assisi. He was a master at teaching Bible lessons with clever props, and a manger scene helped common people relate to the Christmas message more vividly.

In modern-day Rome, you'll find *presepi* all over town—in churches, houses, piazzas, porticos, and even train stations. At Rome's Piazza del Popolo, an annual exhibition features 100 *presepi*, made by artists and schoolchildren. Italians on their evening *passegiata* make a point of strolling from church to church, piazza to piazza, and checking out the various manger scenes.

Some creches are life-size; some are teeny. Some are intricate and beautiful; some are homely. Some are historically accurate, while others have not a hint of ancient Palestine. They might depict Mary dressed in modern clothes in a 21st-century setting, or an Arctic scene with an Eskimo Jesus. From old to avant-garde, each is unique, a window into the imagination of its creator.

Most Italians have a manger scene of their own in their homes. They have a family tradition of adding another figure to the scene each day of the season. On Christmas Eve, the Birthday Boy himself makes his appearance.

The biggest *presepio* is at the Vatican, where a huge Nativity scene is constructed in the center of St. Peter's Square, complete with life-size statues. The most popular *prespio* in Rome is at the Church of Santa Maria in Araco-eli. Its statue of baby Jesus, called the Santo Bambino, is thought to have been carved from olive wood taken from the Garden of Gethsemane, the place where Jesus prayed the night before he was crucified. He's an odd little figure, clothed in rich fabrics and covered with jewels. Children love the Bambino, and write him letters to ask for a favor.

The oldest manger is in Rome's Basilica of Santa Maria Maggiore. There you can see five wooden planks that are said to be 2,000 years old—remnants of the original manger where baby Jesus laid his head all those years ago on the first Christmas Day.

There are large-scale presepi in churches and piazzas and small ones in people's homes.

A FAMILY CHRISTMAS IN SWITZERLAND

High in Switzerland, the mighty Alps seem to shout the glory of God. Up here, where villages huddle under towering peaks, Christmas fills a wintry wonderland with good cheer. Traditions are strong and celebration comes with families, friends, and fun. It may be cold outside, but as the sun sets, it's impossible not to linger in this cozy setting.

I spent a wonderful Christmas in the fairy-tale village of Gimmelwald with my family and my local friend Olle. When Olle's parents came by, they pulled out all the stops to celebrate a traditional Swiss family Christmas.

In Switzerland, the local Santa tramps from house to house bringing treats to the village kids..

My son Andy really got into it. He assumed the role of Samichlaus—the Swiss "St. Nick." Andy's sidekick, the black-clad henchman Schmutzli, was Olle's son, Sven. And the town donkey played himself. By tradition, Samichlaus visits all the homes in town to see which kids have been naughty and nice. The kids sing their Swiss Santa a Christmas carol, and then eagerly dig into his big burlap bag to get their goodies.

The Swiss celebrate other traditions popular in America. They tramp through the snow to cut their own Christmas tree. They host parties of spiced wine and special foods. In Switzerland, it's a fondue party. "When we Swiss plan a cozy party," my friend Olle explained, "on the invitation we add the word 'FIGUGEGL.'" (It's pronounced fee-goo-geck-ul.) It's an acronym that stands for *"Fondu isch guet und git e gueti Lune"*—Fondue is good and gives a good mood. "When you read this," Olle said, "you know a good time is planned."

As Christmas Eve came, we joined the villagers for a hot-spiced wine party in the frigid open air, gathering around a bonfire of flaming tree trunks. Then we went inside and sang Christmas songs around the piano. Grandpa read to us,

Christmas in the Alps brings sleigh rides by torchlight and cozy family gatherings, where grandpa reads the Nativity story from the Bible.

with his weathered fingers holding the dog-eared family Bible—beautiful as a Rembrandt painting, but real and now.

We topped the evening off with a joyful sleigh ride. After riding a lift high above town, we mounted the old-style wooden snow bicycles. Our struggles to master the technology soon turned into hysterical laughter. Then we romped down the mountainside, through a darkness lit only by torches.

CHRISTMAS EVE BUILD-UP

All across Europe, people embrace the coming of Christmas. Christians go to an evening church service. Neo-pagans gather around a roaring bonfire as in days of old. In France, Christmas Eve brings the most anticipated culinary event of the year—*Le Reveillon de Nöel*, or Christmas Eve feast. It's a multicourse affair lasting hours, featuring raw oysters and regional specialties. In Italy, they gather around the home's focal point—not a Christmas tree but their *presepio*, where they add the final figure of Jesus. Then they sit down to a huge meal featuring—not turkey or goose—but eel. (*Buon appetito!*) In Austria, a bell rings, and children enter the room to see their Christmas tree for the first time, already beautifully decorated and surrounded by presents. Then they sing "Silent Night"

Across Europe, the holiday "turkey" takes many forms. In Italy, it's eels; in France, oysters.

(*Stille Nacht*), the carol that originated here. In Norway, kids set out a bowl of porridge—not for Santa—but for the *Julenisse*, a magical elfin creature, who will bring them presents in the morning.

Then the kids go to bed with visions of sugar plums, oysters, and eels dancing in their heads. For a few hours, the world sleeps in peace, until . . .

It's Christmas Day! Dawn breaks, church bells chime, and excited children spring from their beds as the world awakes to the joy of Christmas. Kids open presents and enjoy sweets. In Britain, families pull on "Christmas crackers," which pop open to reveal a fun little toy. Families sit down for more meals and more feasting. It's another Christmas Day, heralding the birth of Jesus. Across Europe,

Whether the big celebration takes place on Christmas Eve or Christmas Day, it always involves a big meal with lots of goodies.

people are wishing their families, friends—and even strangers—the same thing: *Gledelig Jul! Joyeux Noël! Fröliche Weihnachten! Buon Natale!* Merry Christmas!

Whether Christian or pagan, old or young, German or Italian, Christmas is a time when everyone has a reason to celebrate. The feeling of joy, magic, and wonder is universal this time of year. Whether you're strolling through markets, perusing *presepi*, feasting with family, honoring the spirituality of the holiday, enjoying the sparkling lights and colorful decorations, or sledding down alpine slopes, 'tis the season to be grateful. Christmas is perhaps Europe's oldest festival, and it brings the year's calendar of festivals to a joyous conclusion. It's a time to frolic, to look ahead, and also to reflect, celebrating traditions that have been observed since the beginning of time.

The festivities create memories and carry on traditions that will live on for generations.

TRAVELERS' FAVORITES

An Eclectic Mix of Fun

While I've featured my favorite festivals, Europe offers thousands more. I asked my Facebook readers to share their favorites. They submitted an enticing array of parties and I chose the top 30 (listed here in calendar order). Thanks to our guest travel writers.

This mix of celebrations reflects the delightful variety of festivals Europe has to offer. Some are based on a real or legendary medieval event, which may be reenacted as part of the fun (like Fivizzano's Battle of the Archers, Rothenburg's Meistertrunk, and Geneva's Escalade Festival). Other festivals are tinged with patriotism (like King's Day in the Netherlands).

Several festivals are seasonal, celebrating the coming of spring (Valencia's Fallas Festival and Edinburgh's Beltane Fire Festival) or the return of livestock from alpine meadows in fall (Austria's Almabtrieb).

Some festivals honor a Christian saint's day—but even these might have pagan elements, and vary from country to country. The Night of St. John, which falls near the summer solstice, is celebrated with midnight bonfires, gentle head-bonking in Portugal, and scaring off witches in Spain. Dublin's St. Patrick's Festival is more silly than saintly. The most religious festival in the batch is Italy's lovely, ephemeral Festival of Flowers.

Secular entries include parties (Villach's mini-Oktoberfest), lighthearted protests (Venice's Vogalonga), and a celebration of gay pride (Vienna Pride). Others are devoted to edibles—from wine to chocolate. Many festivals focus on the arts: music, dance, film, and artistic creations.

Whether it's crossing a pontoon bridge in Venice or tossing oranges in Ivrea, you're sure to find a festival that appeals to you. For locations, see the map on page 10.

To seek out more celebrations, start with the list of major holidays and festivals at www.ricksteves.com/festivals. Before you plan your trip around a festival, remember that some event dates change from year to year, so be sure to check the website of the festival or local tourist information office.

BATTLE OF THE ORANGES

Festive food fight remembering medieval rivalries

Every February, the northern Italian town of Ivrea hosts the Battle of the Oranges (*Battaglia delle Arance*), drawing thousands of visitors to its old-town center. Some people observe the action behind safety nets, while others join the fray, dodging flying oranges amid horse-drawn carriages and piles of horse manure. Just a short drive from Milan, Ivrea makes an easy day-trip to see this fun, chaotic festival (which lasts three days—Sunday, Monday, and Fat Tuesday). Watch as "soldiers" in horse-drawn carriages and "peasants" on the ground pelt each other with oranges—nearly 500 tons over a three-day period. For around €5, you can purchase a red-stocking cap to mark yourself as a non-combatant, which means that while you may still get hit with a stray fruit here and there, no one (at least in theory) should be aiming directly at you. Note that if you want to participate in the battle, you must be part of a registered team. For more info: storicocarnevaleivrea.it.

Thanks to Hyla Melloy, of Stuttgart, Germany, for her write-up and photo.

FALLAS FESTIVAL

IN VALENCIA, SPAIN, ON MARCH 15-19 (#12 ON MAP)

Street parties and parades of giant mannequins

Celebrated in March, the Fallas Festival (*Las Fallas*) in Valencia honors the coming of spring and sparks a unique attack on the senses. Spectacular displays of fireworks occur daily, with a Valencian twist: You will FEEL the rumble reverberating through your body. Parades with brass bands, traditional costumes, and firecrackers fill the city, culminating in street parties for everyone to enjoy. Aside from the incredible cuisine, from perfect paellas to mouthwatering churros, a highlight is the pilgrimage where more than 50,000 people offer flowers to the Virgin Mary. The festival's name comes from the hundreds of giant statues—sometimes satirical and always astonishing—that are erected across the city as a competition between neighborhoods. It's a beautiful irony to watch them burn brightly in an epic finale, to which you're so close you can feel the flames. For more info, see http://fallespatrimonicomu.info/en.

Thanks to Kerrie Simpson of Manchester, UK, for her write-up, and to Luke Westberg, of Quincy, IL, for the photos.

St. Patrick's Festival

In Dublin, Ireland, on March 17 (#13 on map)

Beer, Irish jigs, and all things green

In Dublin, St. Patrick's Festival lasts four days, and the highlight is the giant parade on March 17. All along the two-mile parade route, revelers sport an assortment of goofy hats and festive face paint. The parade features a quirky conveyor belt of visual and audio stimuli, including school marching bands, giant puppets spidering along the street on long poles, crosier-staff-bearing St. Patricks in flowing green robes anointing the crowds with mock blessings, and colorful floats blowing Lawrence Welk bubbles and swirls of cloudlike foam into the air. The revelry continues long after the parade ends. Bands on outdoor stages churn out lively rhythms laced with fiddle, banjo, and flute. Irish dance troupes featuring lasses in short skirts perform a precision swirl of set dancing as locals break into their own ragged impromptu dance steps, locking elbows and kicking up their heels. For more info, see www.stpatricksfestival.ie.

Thanks to Pat O'Connor, co-author of the *Rick Steves Ireland* guidebook, of Edmonds, WA, for his write-up and photos.

KING'S DAY

National birthday party, celebrating canalside dressed in orange

Every April 27, the Dutch celebrate their bright orange holiday of King's Day, or *Koningsdag*, in celebration of the birthday of their monarch, Willem-Alexander. The Dutch have a tradition of *Oranjegeket* (going orange crazy), because orange is their proud and loud national color. Never is this more apparent than in the clothes, wigs, big hats, and bright feather boas prominent throughout the partying, wandering masses on King's Day. While King's Day is a nationwide holiday, it's estimated that a million Dutch converge on the capital city of Amsterdam for parties, bands, flea markets, and most significantly, the parade of brightly-colored boats cruising up and down the city's famed canals, playing loud music and showing off before the jolly masses on the quaysides. So grab a beer or two, dip your fries in mayo, and join the orange crowd in Amsterdam this April.

Thanks to Steven McIntire of Alameda, CA, for his write-up and photo (on the left) and to Dominic Arizona Bonuccelli for the photo on the right.

BELTANE FIRE FESTIVAL

Pagans dancing around roaring bonfires

Wind your way up Edinburgh's iconic Calton Hill, guided by the flickering light of torches and the sounds of revelry. What greets you at the top is the Beltane Fire Festival, and a night you'll never forget. Held every year on April 30, this ancient-Celtic-inspired festival has run since the 1980s, and tells the story of the awakening of the May Queen and the rebirth of the Green Man. Expect to see half-naked, painted bodies dance and perform in a procession across the top of the hill. As they cheer and shout, watch out for the twirling of flames and torches all around you. The culmination of the festivities ends with a roaring bonfire, whose warmth will leave you yearning for the approaching summer that the festival beckons. For more info, see https://beltane.org.

Thanks to Emily Gwiazda of Caledon, Ontario, for her write-up and photo (on the right) and to ©Coreross | Dreamstime.com for the photo on the left.

Tree Blossom Festival

In Werder, Germany, in early May (#16 on map)

*Enjoying local fruit wines
amid flowering trees*

When I heard about the *Baumblütenfest*, the fruit wine festival near Berlin held the first week of May, I couldn't wait to hear more. Then I heard more: Rowdy trains full of drunk teens—all in pursuit of locally produced fruit wines. But *Baumblütenfest* (Tree Blossom Festival) is worth the one-hour trip. That chaotic train ride transports you from the capital city to the countryside. Walking with hordes from the station, you're struck by the tranquility, with greenery and flowering trees stretching to the Havel River. The stillness is broken by the vendors' stands. Plastic cups soon litter the streets. Goofy hats and charmless knick-knacks are for sale. Ignore that. You're here for the wine.

Stachelbeere (gooseberry) and *Johannisbeere* (currant) are transformed by crazy homemade contraptions into wine. Continue past the crowds and rides, bringing your bottle to the edge of the island. Sit in the grass. Gaze at the water. Drink up. *Baumblütenfest* is a mouthful, but it gets easier to say as the fruit wine flows. For more info, see www.werder-havel.de.

Thanks to Erin "ebe" Porter of Berlin, Germany, for her write-up and photo.

FESTIVAL OF FLOWERS

THROUGHOUT ITALY, DURING MAY AND JUNE (#17 ON MAP)

Street-size mosaics made of flowers

Leave it to the Italians to take something Mother Nature has perfected and make it even more breathtaking. That's exactly what happens every May and June at the *Infiorata*—the Festival of Flowers. Vibrant blooms are harvested and used in fresh, dried, natural, and dyed forms to create mosaic masterpieces all over Italy. The sweet fragrance of the pillowy petals carpet the path for religious processions all the way to the altar.

Each of the hundreds of *Infiorata* festivals has a unique identity, giving travelers a window into what matters most in each region. The one thing they all have in common is that the religious scenes are literally swept away within hours of completion, leaving every witness with the knowledge that beauty comes from the creative act, not the completed product. Because it is fleeting, this festival leaves a lasting impression on those who experience its glory.

Thanks to Colleen Mariotti of Bainbridge Island, WA, for her write-up and to © Salvo77na | Dreamstime for the photo.

Meistertrunk Festival

Medieval soldiers parading and heroically chugging local wine

Georg Nusch, mayor of 17th-century Rothenburg, purportedly drained over three liters of wine in one incredible gulp, after an invading general promised to spare the town if the mayor could down the drink. Nusch not only saved Rothenburg from destruction, he gave birth to the legend known as *Der Meistertrunk* (The Master Draught). It's celebrated every year with a four-day festival that falls on the weekend of Pentecost (usually in early June or late May). The festival takes tiny Rothenburg, already one of Germany's most well-preserved medieval towns, back to 1631. Hundreds of locals don dramatic period costumes as soldiers, merchants, and townsfolk to recreate the events leading up to Nusch's dizzying feat. The celebration takes place in and outside of Rothenburg's medieval walls with an open-air play; military parades featuring pounding drums, battle songs, and intimidating weaponry; military camps with crackling fires and horse-drawn carts; and food, drink, and live modern music at night. For more info, see http://en.meistertrunk.de.

Thanks to Nick Medina of Chicago, IL, for his write-up and photo.

Vogalonga

In Venice, Italy, in late May or early June (#19 on map)

A "protest-ival" of rowing contests in colorful garb

In 1973, in protest against the mechanized boats harming the lagoon habitat and the historic buildings of Venice and the Veneto, a group of friends took up arms—in the form of oars—and created a noncompetitive race, using traditional Venetian forward-rowing boats. The protest festival continues 40 years on, held on Pentecost Sunday. These days, time-honored, flat-bottom, small boats like the *sandolo*, *macareta*, and *s'ciopon* are joined by modern-day kayaks as well as larger vessels like the *peata*, which holds about 16 rowers. At the sound of a shotgun, local and worldwide rowing enthusiasts alike make their way through a 30 kilometer- (19 mile-) course through the shallow canals of the lagoon. As they oar their way along the Venetian waterways, wide-eyed onlookers perched on banks and bridges spiritedly cheer for the colorful aquatic parade of thousands of human-powered watercraft. For more info, see vogalonga.com.

Thanks to Trish Feaster of Edmonds, WA, for her write-up and photo.

DecorAction

In Madrid, Spain, in mid-June (#20 on map)

Arts and decorated facades in a neighborhood

Filled with color, texture and creativity—from the beautiful to the funky—Madrid's *DecorAcción* celebrates art, design, and decoration. Each June, this four-day street festival lights up the Barrio de las Letras neighborhood with amazing art installations on the facades of building after building, while pop-up shops selling antiques and vintage fare line the streets. Whimsically decorated residential balconies and colorful pennants hang over the streets, creating a canopy that expands the festival to the sky. Locals and visitors can take workshops on topics such as creating a personal tablescape, Japanese writing, and trends in floral arranging. Wander into neighborhood restaurants to check out the decorated patios for a total dining experience. The festival is a full-on, five-sense feast for the creative mind, vintage shopper, and the traveler looking for a unique, easy to access, local experience. For more info, see http://decoraccion.nuevo-estilo.es.

Thanks to Shawn Elizabeth Personke of Chelsea, MI, for her write-up and to Rosa Gutierrez for the photo.

VIENNA PRIDE

LGBTQ parades and balls benefiting AIDS

Of all of its magnificent balls, Vienna's most fabulous by far is Europe's largest AIDS benefit event: the Life Ball, held on Rathausplatz. Since 1992, this enthralling celebration has drawn dozens of celebrities to the Austrian capital to raise funding and awareness for AIDS/HIV research, treatment, and prevention programs. What makes this event spectacular year after year is its unbridled celebration of life, thrillingly evident in the competition of glittering, feathered, sequined costumes and its determinedly inclusive atmosphere. The glad rags come off at the end of Pride Week as Vienna's Rainbow Parade closes out the festivities with a joyous, colorful—and scantily clad—march around the capital's downtown Ringstrasse. This is an opportunity to both acknowledge the hard-won victories of a centuries-long struggle for LGBTQ rights and to reaffirm the ongoing fight for equality. In years past, Pride Village has even hosted a Hangover Breakfast the following morning, including the crowning of this year's Dirndl Queen and Lederhosen King. For more info, see http://viennapride.at.

Thanks to Gretl Satorius of Vienna, Austria, for her write-up, to Tobe Mayr for the photo on the left, and to ©Digitalpress | Dreamstime.com for the photo on the right.

Bloomsday Festival

In Dublin, Ireland, on June 16 (#22 on map)

James Joyce literary pub crawl

Even those unfamiliar with James Joyce will delight in the wacky sports, eccentric costumes, and tasty treats of Dublin's Bloomsday Festival. It honors author James Joyce and Leopold Bloom, the lead character in Joyce's novel, *Ulysses*. Throughout the streets of Dublin, actors recite dramatic and silly readings from *Ulysses*, often prompting cheers and shouts from the crowd. You can also partake in the Joycean pub crawl if that strikes your fancy. Or you can even crawl into bed. Molly's Bed (named for Molly Bloom, Leopold's wife) is a full-size bed in the middle of the street where festival-goers can take a photo, or perhaps a nap. While any attire is just fine, try to find a local charity shop (thrift shop) and support an Irish charity while picking up a feathered hat, fancy pearls, or other Edwardian garb to immerse yourself in the festivities. For more info, see www.bloomsdayfestival.ie.

Thanks to Claire Pfarr of Pittsburgh, PA, for her write-up and to Pat O'Connor for the photos.

MUSIC FESTIVAL

IN PARIS, FRANCE, ON JUNE 21 (#23 ON MAP)

Music in countless venues across town

My favorite European festival happens in Paris every year on the evening of the summer solstice, June 21. Called *Fête de la Musique*, it started in Paris in 1982 and is now celebrated in many cities in Europe as Worldwide Music Day. All over Paris, streets are closed to traffic and pedestrians wander around freely, listening to live music and enjoying street food sold from carts. Some indoor venues are open for special concerts. Most, if not all, are free to the public. Many bars and restaurants have special menus. Even the public transport system gets into the act: RATP sells a special discounted ticket that is good all night, and the Métro, bus, and suburban train lines continue service until the wee hours. It's a lot of fun if you happen to be in Paris that day! For more info, see www.fetedelamusique.de/en.

Thanks to John M of Milwaukee, WI, for his write-up and to Claude Thibault / Alamy Stock Photo for the photo.

St. John Festival

Sardines, port, and head-bonking

Not well known beyond Portugal, Porto stages an annual festival on June 23 which is second to none! The celebration, *Festa de São João do Porto*, honors their most revered saint, St. John the Baptist. Dating back six centuries, the festival blends Christianity with old pagan rites: grilled sardines, lots of port and wine, balloon lanterns, midnight fireworks, and jumping over bonfires. Musicians fill the streets on the Douro riverfront. Don't be surprised if a stalk of leeks or a clove of garlic suddenly thwacks you on the head. It's just the locals' way of wishing you good luck. Better yet, they bonk people on their heads with soft plastic hammers that beep—that's the coolest! No one is immune from the bonking, from babies in strollers to the elderly with walkers. If you dare...go for the beeping hammer lines. It is great "beeping" fun!

Thanks to Randy Ratzlaff of Terrell, TX, for his write-up and photo.

NIGHT OF ST. JOHN

Sardines, beer, and scaring off witches

Noche de San Juan (Night of St. John) is a festival celebrated on June 23 throughout different parts of Spain, but it's best in this autonomous community of Galicia. At night, residents light hundreds of bonfires on the beaches to ward off evil and witches. You can walk through the old city of A Coruña to see streets lined with large grills fuming smoke and releasing the savory scent of grilled sardines. Families and friends enjoy *cañas* (beers) and endless amounts of sardines from plastic plates. When the sun sets, the lighting of the fires begins and the entire city is overrun with a thick fog of smoke and ashes. Before the night is over, for good luck, you must jump over the bonfire seven times and scream "*Meigas fora!*" (Witches off!). For more info, see www.hoguerassanjuan.com.

Thanks to Angelo Ramos of A Coruña, Spain, for his write-up and photos.

LIGHTS OF BEAUNE

World-class wines, cuisine, and light shows

While Beaune might be best known for the taste of its Burgundian cuisine and delectable wines from nearby vineyards, summer visitors know that a late-evening walk through the town excites another sense: sight. Dotted throughout the walled French city are historic buildings whose facades become nightly canvases for dazzling digital light shows, called *Lumières à Beaune*. With state-of-the-art animations and projections, each venue tells a different visual story from Beaune's and France's past, highlighting famous citizens, the humble lives of ordinary people, and intricate landscapes and architecture. Residents and visitors of all ages share in this communal experience as they go from one location to the next, delighting in this rich, kaleidoscopic spectacle.

Thanks to Trish Feaster of Edmonds, WA, for her write-up and photo.

KARLOVY VARY INTERNATIONAL FILM FESTIVAL

IN KARLOVY VARY, CZECH REPUBLIC, IN EARLY JULY (#27 ON MAP)

International films and red-carpet events

Berlin, London, Cannes...Karlovy Vary? Film festivals in Europe are fun and exciting—and they increase your awareness of the world! My favorite is held in July in the beautiful, historic city of Karlovy Vary in the Czech Republic. Over the course of nine days, more than 150 international movies are presented, including dozens of world premieres! Often, the actors and directors attend the screenings and speak to the audience at the conclusion, adding to people's enjoyment and understanding of the films. In addition to the films, all of which are in English or subtitled, there are celebrations along the river, on the red carpet, and throughout the city. The Czechs really love their cinema and the festival is wonderful, especially the cheap ticket prices (about $4), lodging, and tasty food! For more info, see www.kviff.com/en/homepage.

Thanks to Melanie Sims Leon of Hohenfels, Germany, for her write-up and to ©Josefkubes | Dreamstime.com for the photo.

Gărâna Jazz Festival

High-quality jazz in rustic mountain village

The Gărâna Jazz Festival in Romania has all the ingredients of a hidden gem. Held high up in the woods of the Carpathian Mountains outside the town of Gărâna, this four-day festival brings together a genre-bending mix of jazz musicians from around the world. You'll hear everything from traditional trumpet and sax acts, to symphonic ensembles pushing the envelope of their tradition, to DJs giving it the electronic spin. From unknowns to Oscar winners, all the acts are impressive, and the audience, clued into the privilege of being there, is definitely into them. Up to 10,000 people attend each year, but it doesn't feel crowded—there's plenty of space to sit on the cozy wooden benches, carved from the trees the local timber industry sustainably produces. And for those brisk mountains nights, the delicious soups and delicacies the chefs serve morning to night are simply divine. For more info, see garana-jazz.ro.

Thanks to Matthew Paffhouse of McBain, MI, for his write-up and to Radu Condrea for the photo.

Bohemia Jazz Fest

In Prague, Czech Republic, in mid-July (#29 on map)

*Laid-back jazz in atmospheric
Old Town Square*

Jazz lovers, it's time to plan a trip to Prague! The Old Town Square boasts free open-air concerts for two days in mid-July. Whether you enjoy classic jazz, swing, or blues—or a hybrid of the three—it's absolutely one of the best laid-back jazz parties Europe can offer. Food and drink vendors line the stage, so grab a beer, a hot pastry lovingly spun over flame and sprinkled with sugar, grilled chicken or sausage, and enjoy the numerous performers—a great mix of instrumentalists and vocalists. If you get up to dance, chances are you'll find many willing to join you. Located near the historical astronomical clock and St. Nicholas Church, it's easy to find and a great way to mix sightseeing and entertainment. For more info, see www.bohemiajazzfest.cz/en.

Thanks to Jennifer Martin of Port Townsend, WA, for her write-up and to ©Rozmaryna | Dreamstime.com for the photo.

Battle of the Archers

In Fivizzano, Italy, in mid-July (#30 on map)

Medieval Tuscan archery contest

Every July, nestled in the lush hills of northern Tuscany, the sleepy walled town of Fivizzano travels back in time. A medieval archery competition, *Disfida degli Arcieri di Terra e di Corte* (Battle of the Archers between the Countryside and Court), has taken place on the same square, Piazza Medicea, for 500 years. Attracting thousands of witnesses to this fun, fierce rivalry between the town and nearby villages, the event is an elaborate and boisterous affair as locals show off their proud tradition. The weekend begins by setting the scene with a medieval food market, games, music, and animals. Sunday's sunset introduces each rival group—the costumed marchers with drums and impressive banners parade beautifully through the streets. As the warm cobblestones cool, the archery competition starts, fervent and engaging; a hush falls over the audience at every mark taken. Stunning performances such as flag throwing and fire dancing are interspersed throughout. If you're lucky, you'll join a great party by following the victors to their favorite bar.

Thanks to Ella Weehuizen of Russell, New Zealand, for her write-up and photo.

LUDWIGSBURG FESTIVAL
CLASSIC OPEN AIR & FIREWORKS

IN LUDWIGSBURG, GERMANY, IN MID-JULY (#31 ON MAP)

Lite classical music with picnics and fireworks

Imagine watching shimmers of fireworks bounce off a lakeside palace while a live orchestra plays in the background. That's exactly what you'll find every July at the Ludwigsburg Festival, held on a Saturday evening at Seeschloss Monrepos, near Stuttgart, Germany. The best seating is on the hillside of the lawn—if you're quick enough to claim a spot for yourself. Some sit on blankets; some turn this into the celebration of the year and bring folding tables, linens, flowers, champagne, and candelabras. Families can bring outdoor toys, and many people bring wine, fresh bread, and cheese. German sausage, beer, and wine is available for purchase. The orchestra often plays popular movie theme songs to add humor, making the evening light and fun. A hotel on the property allows you to turn this affair into a weekend getaway. Fair warning: This may certainly become the event you plan your future vacations around.

Thanks to Jennifer Martin of Port Townsend, WA, for her write-up and photo.

REDENTORE FESTIVAL

In Venice, Italy, later in July (#32 on map)

Pontoon bridge across canal, lit by fireworks

Just follow the crowds and you'll be in a perfect spot for the *Festa del Redentore* in Venice. It's a festival to give thanks for the end of the plague in 1576. Held on the third weekend in July, the highlight is a spectacular show of fireworks that lights up the sky over the Grand Canal and the Il Redentore church on the island of Giudecca. Go out early to find a place to sit. The locals will show you where, and stop when they stop. Snack on pizza and a bottled bellini while waiting for the fireworks that happen at nightfall. On the days before and after the fireworks, you can literally walk on water on a temporary pontoon bridge from Venice to Giudecca.

Thanks to Tiffani Sherman of Dunedin, FL, for her write-up and to ©Delstudio | Dreamstime.com for the photo.

Cosmo Jazz Festival

Très cool *tunes in chic alpine town*

If you want to combine your love of music with the thrill of the great outdoors, make your way to Chamonix during the last week of July. Musicians from all corners of the globe share their talents *en plein aire* at venues in the chic valley town of Chamonix and at altitudes with dizzying French alpine and glacial panoramas. Impromptu performances can happen when and where you least expect it—along a hiking trail, atop a boulder, or even in a cable car thousands of feet above the valley floor. From midday until late into the night, you'll hear and feel this unforgettable mixture of melody and Mother Nature, where the hills really are alive with the sound of music. For more info, see www.cosmojazzfestival.com/en.

Thanks to Trish Feaster of Edmonds, WA, for her write-up and photo (right) and to Reini4810 | Dreamstime.com for the photo on the left.

Sighişoara Medieval Festival

In Sighişoara, Romania, in late July (#34 on map)

Medieval wenches, knaves, and troubadours in quirky old village

Romania's Sighişoara Medieval Festival is a must-see destination for anyone harboring a penchant for medieval parties in historically spooky towns. Great for kids and adults of all ages, the festivities include costumed parades through winding cobblestone streets, live theater performances, dancing, concerts, and hands-on activities. After lunch at one of the food carts or restaurants, try your hand at archery or visit the blacksmith's tower. Follow the sounds of the lute player to find imprisoned witches and jailed law-breakers serving their sentences. If you feel left out in plain street clothes, don't worry; simply rent a costume and join in the festivities. Cap off your experience with a tour of the house where Dracula was born, conveniently located in the middle of the festival. Sighişoara is easily accessible by train, and the festival is held in the old town, on the last weekend of July.

Thanks to Jennifer Martin of Port Townsend, WA, for her write-up and photo.

Edinburgh Festival

In Edinburgh, Scotland, in August (#35 on map)

World-class music, dance, theater, and comedy—plus bagpipes

In August a riot of overlapping festivals known collectively as the Edinburgh Festival rages simultaneously. The official Edinburgh International Festival is the original, with music, dance, drama and more (major events sell out well in advance). The less formal Fringe Festival, featuring edgy comedy and theater, is huge—with 2,000 shows—and has eclipsed the original festival in popularity (half-price tickets for some events are sold on the day of the show). The Military Tattoo is a massing of bands, drums, and bagpipes, with groups from all over the former British Empire. Displaying military finesse with a stirring lone-piper finale, this grand spectacle fills the Castle Esplanade (book ahead). Every day is jammed with formal and spontaneous fun. Many city sights run on extended hours. It's a glorious time to be in Edinburgh...if you have (and can afford) a room. Plan ahead; book ahead. For more info, see www.edinburgh festivals.co.uk.

Thanks to Bob T. Bruce of Edmonds, WA, for his write-up and to Dominic Arizona Bonuccelli for the photo.

Villacher Church Day Festival

Oompah music, sausages, and beer without the Oktoberfest craziness

Villach's Church Day (*Villacher Kirchtag*) festival is a mix between Munich's Oktoberfest and traditional May Day celebrations in the US. The town of Villach has an idyllic setting on the River Drau, with a hilltop castle, Burg Landskron, overlooking the picturesque valley. A nice walk up to the castle, which has a view restaurant at the top, allows for a pleasant respite from the activity of the festival. During the week-long festival, Villach welcomes an estimated 400,000 visitors, many wearing traditional

lederhosen and dirndl. It's a celebration for all ages, with amusement park rides intermixed with beer, food, and souvenir tents. Each restaurant sets up their own tent with an accompanying oompah band, and nighttime brings DJs to the Kaiser-Josef-Platz for the Kirchtag Disco, where the young gather each night. The Kirchtag festival, smaller and tamer than Munich's big bash, welcomes tourists who want an Oktoberfest experience, but maybe have a tighter budget. For more info, see villacherkirchtag.at.

Thanks to Bob Grant of Bellmawr, NJ, for his write-up and photo.

FESTIVAL OF GRÀCIA

IN BARCELONA, SPAIN, IN MID-AUGUST (#37 ON MAP)

Neighborhoods competing for most creatively decorated street

If you find yourself in Barcelona during mid-August, check out one of the world's most colorful and energetic week-long block parties. For nearly 200 years, the *Festa Major de Gràcia* has attracted those interested in seeing which neighborhood street will win the annual prize as "best decorated." The elaborate, immense, and colorful scenes constructed by the locals must be seen to be believed. Some can even be experienced, as is the case with this walk-through underwater artistic explosion from 2013 (pictured). Modestly priced food and drink, free live music, and large, enthusiastic crowds round out this unforgettable local experience. For more info, see www.festamajordegracia.cat.

Thanks to John Meglino of Brooklyn, NY, for his write-up and photo.

ALMABTRIEB FESTIVAL

IN MAYRHOFEN, AUSTRIA, IN EARLY OCTOBER (#38 ON MAP)

*Well-dressed herds, and partying
till the cows come home*

For Austrians, this event is a normal part of alpine life in many villages, but for others, it's a beautiful, other-worldly celebration that many flock to see from around the world. It's known as the *Almabtrieb*, or Cows Come Home, and the largest of these festivals is held on the first Saturday of October in Mayrhofen, Austria, in the Tirol region of the Alps. Some 180,000 steer, horses, sheep, and goats make their way down from the mountains where they've spent the summer grazing the lush fields. In this region, many animals are decorated with  stunning flower crowns and colorful garlands and wear hand-painted bells. You can hear the bells as the shepherds herd the animals down to their stables. This free event is absolutely one celebration not to be missed!

Thanks to Megan Haigood of Stuttgart, Germany, for her write-up and photo.

Eurochocolate Festival

In Perugia, Italy, in mid-October (#39 on map)

Chocolate, chocolate, chocolate. Nuff said.

Imagine the quaint streets of a pristine medieval Italian town lined with hundreds of vendors selling chocolate. For 10 days every October, Perugia—the home of Baci Chocolates—turns into a sweet tooth's paradise during the largest chocolate festival in Europe. From chocolate made by old Italian men, to the world's largest chocolate bar at the end of a GIANT selfie stick, Eurochocolate gives you a unique view on modern Italian culture. A festival that turns only 24 this year, it's a spectacular way to gorge on a gift from the heavens. Tickets for a "Chocopass" are relatively inexpensive (some are around €6), and come with a heaping of free chocolate, chocolate-inspired things, and other goodies. Don't trip on the cobblestones as you make your way to the city's spectacular panoramic viewpoint, munching on all the chocolate goodies—both domestic and international—the festival has to offer.

Thanks to Sydney Zaruba of Saint Augustine, FL, for her write-up and to Maurice Joseph / Alamy Stock Photo for the photo.

Escalade Festival

Reenactment of historic battle, with torches and bonfires

Geneva's *Fête de l'Escalade*, held on the second weekend of December, commemorates the night in 1602 when the scrappy townsfolk defeated the Duke of Savoy, who wanted to capture the then-independent and wealthy city-state. On Saturday, to recreate parts of the nighttime battle, there are tours of secret passageways in the Old Town, mock sword fights, and cannon-firing demonstrations. The festival culminates with a big parade on Sunday night, with scores of men dressed as soldiers of the Savoy, wearing helmets and some riding on horseback. The way is lit by torches of real fire. The parade ends in the square in front of the cathedral, where an enormous bonfire is lit. And what Swiss festival is complete without chocolate? The symbol is a chocolate soup pot, a weapon of the battle's heroine. Every family buys one to smash and eat at home. For more info, see www.1602.ch.

Thanks to Stephen H. Padre of Washington, D.C., for his write-up and photo.

ABOUT *RICK STEVES'*
EUROPEAN FESTIVALS

THIS BOOK is the companion of the public television special, *Rick Steves' European Festivals.* If you've enjoyed this book, you'll love the show, which puts you right in the middle of the festival action. You can see the show on your local public television station or any time at ricksteves.com, where it's streamable for free, along with the rest of my series and my specials on Easter and Christmas (which each have companion books, too).

While this book is based on the *European Festivals* TV script, it offers more depth. During the filming of these festivals, we learned far more than we could fit into the public television show, because we're limited to only 6,000 words for a one-hour show. To share that additional information, I am thankful to have this book.

The *European Festivals* special was many years in the making. I realized that over the years we had filmed many of Europe's top festivals for our public television series. In 2015, I collected all of the festival segments we had already shot: Carnevale, Holy Week, Easter, Sevilla's Spring Fair, Pamplona's Running of the Bulls, Bastille Day in Paris, and Christmas. Then, in 2016, we topped it off by shooting Siena's Palio, Munich's Oktoberfest, and the Highland Games in Airth, Scotland. That gave us just the right variety and content to make an hour-long special. In 2017, we wove it all together and produced our show and this book.

In line with our goal of teaching—through our travel classes, guidebooks, and public television shows—we do our best to give the context for each festival and to explore its historic and cultural roots. We were fortunate to have expert, enthusiastic help from my guide friends in Europe. They welcomed us into their towns and homes, tirelessly filled us with information, helped us get permission from local authorities, and secured for us the best vantage points for filming the action as it thundered by. They got us a seat at the table for all that intimate family fun, making sure we tried all the tasty holiday treats and drank that liquid holiday good cheer. It's connecting with people that distinguishes a good trip, and it was certainly our friends that helped us connect with people at each festival, enabling us to get so much out of each party.

I'd also like to thank others who were instrumental in our work: Producer Simon Griffith is with me for every minute of our filming in Europe, and then oversees the post-production work with our artful TV editor, Steve Cammarano. Our tireless cameramen, Peter Rummel and Karel Bauer, are an inspiration for their commitment to the quality of our public television work. Gene Openshaw, who wrote most of this book, expertly took the raw material from the script and used his own vast store of travel experience and general smarts to fill these easy-to-read pages. Many thanks as well to Risa Laib for editing, to Sandra Hundacker for managing the art, and to Dave Hoerlein for providing the graphics.

Finally, kudos to our hardworking friends at Avalon Travel Publishing, who turned our words and photos into the beautiful book you're holding in your hands.

By providing a little insight into Europe's fascinating festival scene, we hope you'll be inspired to seek out your own top 10 favorites and to borrow some of Europe's traditions to enliven your own festivities. All of us here wish you the heartiest of celebrations and—very simply—more joy. To life!

Photo Credits

.

Avalon Travel
Hachette Book Group
1700 Fourth Street
Berkeley, CA 94710

Text © 2017 by Rick Steves' Europe, Inc. All rights reserved.
Maps © 2017 by Rick Steves' Europe, Inc. All rights reserved.
Printed in Canada by Friesens.
First printing November 2017.

ISBN 978-1-63121-799-9
First Edition

For the latest on Rick's talks, guidebooks, Europe tours, public radio show, free audio tours, and public television series, contact Rick Steves' Europe, 130 Fourth Avenue North, Edmonds, WA 98020, 425/771-8303, www.ricksteves.com, rick@ricksteves.com.

Rick Steves' Europe
Writer: Gene Openshaw
Editor: Risa Laib
Graphic Content Director: Sandra Hundacker
Maps & Graphics: David C. Hoerlein
Cover Design: Rhonda Pelikan and Gopa & Ted2, Inc.

Avalon Travel
Senior Editor and Series Manager: Madhu Prasher
Editor: Jamie Andrade
Associate Editor: Sierra Machado
Editorial Intern: Rachael Sablik
Copy Editor: Maggie Ryan
Proofreader: Janet Walden
Production & Typesetting: Gopa & Ted2, Inc.

If you like this book, you'll love...

Rick Steves' Europe: The Specials Collection

To join Rick at each of his top 10 festivals featured in this book, watch his one-hour public television special, *Rick Steves' European Festivals*. This and six more one-hour Rick Steves TV specials fill a two-disc DVD set with lots of vivid travel experiences. Along with European Festivals, this Specials Collection includes *Luther and the Reformation; Iran; The Holy Land; European Christmas; European Easter;* and *Symphonic Journey.* (And, just for giggles, there's a long and embarrassing reel of Rick's bloopers.)

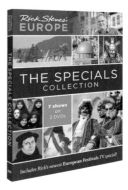

Prefer to stream? All of Rick's TV specials—plus all 100 episodes of the *Rick Steves' Europe* public television series—are available to watch on demand, free at ricksteves.com.

Rick Steves' Europe 101: History & Art for the Traveler

Written in a breezy, humorous style, Rick's *Europe 101* book takes you on a fun and practical sweep through the story of Europe from the Pyramids to Picasso. After decades of tour guiding experience, Rick knows what you need to know—and, just as importantly, what you don't need to know—to get the most out of your sightseeing. Designed for smart people who were sleeping in their art and history classes before they knew they were Europe-bound, this 500-page book brings the art and history of Europe to life to make your travels even more rewarding.

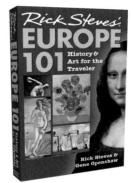

Find these (and lots more) at ricksteves.com